Contents

Introduction 6

1 **Choosing a cat** 8

2 **The perfect kitten** 30

3 **The adult cat** 58

4 **Good cat behaviour** 86

5 **Healthcare** 136

Need to know more? 188

Index 190

Introduction

Cats are now the most popular pets, and it is not surprising that they have overtaken dogs in the popularity stakes. They are small, relatively silent, economical to keep, exercise themselves, easy to feed, and are ideal companions for a wide range of people, from the elderly to those who are out at work all day.

House cats and free-roaming hunters

Whether you want an ordinary moggie or an expensive pedigree cat, the principles of ownership and looking after them are the same. As an increasing number of owners live in big cities and small, high-rise apartment blocks, house cats are becoming more widespread. Although they may not be allowed outside like their free-roaming, predatory cousins, they share a common ancestry and owning a cat of any description is like having a relatively wild creature living with you in your home. Domestication is anathema to many cats who prefer to think that they are independent animals, under the control of nobody but themselves.

Breeding and evolution

To fully appreciate the mystery of the cat, it is necessary to understand how they have evolved to become our tolerant and affectionate companions. Despite the process of selective breeding, today's cats show very little variation in size and shape although they come in an amazing range of coat colours and patterns. There has been some debate over the origins of the domestic cat but it is generally accepted that the African Wild Cat (*Felis lybica*) is the direct ancestor of our modern pets. Cats have been tamed and domesticated for centuries, firstly in their role as hunters and rodent controllers before becoming our much-loved companions. Whatever cat you own, a fireside familiar or an intrepid, fearless hunter, he will have his own unique character and personality. This book will show you how to care for him and build a mutually satisfying relationship between you, which will last a lifetime.

1 Choosing a cat

Choosing a cat suggests that the decision
to keep a pet cat is always part of a carefully
thought-out process which is then followed
by a visit to a local breeder or rescue centre.
However, in a world where cat populations
are expanding fast, this is not always the case.
It may not even be possible for you to choose
between a cat and a kitten as sometimes one
or the other will find your family!

What sort of cat?

When choosing your cat (rather than him choosing you), there are a number of factors that need to be taken into consideration. Cats, regardless of their breed, do not vary too much in size but they do range widely in shape and temperament.

If you don't have a lot of time to spare, it is better to acquire a shorthaired cat which, unlike a longhair, will not need grooming more than twice weekly.

Body shapes

There are a number of basic body shapes to choose from, of which two, muscular and cobby cats, are recognized by most experts. Cat breeds can also be divided into two main categories according to their coat length: shorthaired and longhaired. It is this aspect of cat physiology that can significantly affect many owners because of the potential for allergies and the differences in grooming requirements.

Grooming and allergies

One of the most important decisions to make when choosing a cat is to consider whether you want to own a shorthaired rather than a longhaired one. The latter will definitely need extensive brushing and grooming on a daily basis if its coat is not to become matted and difficult to clean. If some members of your family suffer from dust and hair allergies, they may find themselves more affected by a longhaired cat. This important aspect of cat ownership is worth your consideration because although some people are allergic to all cats, most of them are especially allergic to longhaired ones. In contrast, shorthaired cats will normally affect only those individuals who are extremely allergic to cat hairs.

Before deciding to acquire a longhaired cat, make sure that no members of your family are allergic to them and check out whether anyone has an allergy to skin dander. It is essential for everyone who will come into contact with your new pet to handle a cat before taking on your own. This is to establish that allergic reactions are not going to occur.

Longhaired cats will require about 20 minutes of grooming at least three times a week, if not daily, in order to keep their coats knot-free and in good condition. If you cannot guarantee the time to provide a cat with this amount of brushing and combing attention, then it is always much better to choose a shorthaired variety which will require less grooming time (see pages 64–65).

Colour and sensitivity

The colour of cat that you select can have a rather surprising effect on individuals who are likely to show an allergy to them. In some recent research,

must know

Temperament
It is sometimes said that a cat's coat colour gives us an indication of its personality. Ginger cats are reputed to be gentle and laid-back, whereas tortoiseshells are fiery and tabbies are good hunters. However, this has never been proven.

A longhaired cat, such as this magnificent Persian, will require intensive grooming on a regular basis, preferably every day.

doctors looked at mild to moderate sufferers of
allergic rhinitis and compared cat owners with
people who did not own a cat. The researchers
looked at cat owners without allergies and studied
their cats. Cats kept in or out of the bedroom proved
not to influence the eventual results. However,
perhaps rather surprisingly, those people keeping
a dark-haired cat were seventy-five per cent more
likely to display allergic symptoms than were those
owners with a light-haired cat. Although the reason
for this is currently unknown, it may be linked to the
thickness or composition of the hairs.

Testing for allergy
It is always an excellent idea to arrange for those
members of your family with suspect allergies to
encounter some cats prior to introducing one into
your home. British shorthaired cats, especially the
black and black-and-white varieties, are one of the
most popular cat breeds in the United Kingdom
today, and it is these types of cat that you are most
likely to own if your budget does not allow for
owning a pedigree cat.

Look at your lifestyle
Finally, it is very important when you are making
a breed selection, to choose the variety of cat that
would seem most likely to fit in with your personal
lifestyle and that of your family. For example, you
should never consider keeping a cat that is going
to require a great deal of companionship, such as a
Siamese, if you and your family work and are out of
the house for most of the day. Think carefully about
the sort of cat you want and why you want one.

Pedigree or moggie?

It is possible to invest large sums of money when you are buying a pedigree cat. Indeed, some champion 'show winners', rare breeds and top breeding stock can cost far more than expensive flat screen televisions, computers and music systems.

Pedigree breeds

True pedigree cats are bred to the standards that are published by relevant organizations, and they will have splendid coats and distinctively beautiful eyes which are correctly coloured.

It is probably a myth that top pedigree cats might be termed 'aristocratic' with their specific tastes in home and dietary requirements. However, once you have invested a great deal of money in an expensive pedigree kitten, your commitment to its welfare will undoubtedly increase.

One valuable aspect of opting for a pedigree cat is that it is usually possible to predict the breed quality that you have obtained, particularly when it is an adult. There are other show and pet quality types, and the price range will reflect the potential show winner over the cat that simply 'shows off' on your lap.

You can decide to buy either an expensive pedigree cat, such as the Siamese (above), or you may opt for an ordinary moggie (left). A non-pedigree can have free access to your garden.

Finding your cat

Your veterinary surgeon will advise you about local cat breeders and which have good standards and a genuine interest in the well-being of the kittens they offer for sale. Recommendation is often the best method of locating a respected breeder.

Finding a breeder

Breeders with the highest standards in temperament and physiology will sell their kittens at a premium price. However, it is often best to buy from these breeders because they offer happy, healthy kittens. Professional breeders may only sell kittens at certain times of the year, and if they produce top-quality popular cat breeds of showing standard, they often have a waiting list of potential clients.

Pet shops

It is not wise to purchase a kitten from a pet shop or a large store. Litters of kittens will have been passed on either by people who have them as a result of an accidental mating by their pet, or by commercial breeders whose primary motivation is making a profit. Kittens in pet shops may well have suffered from an interruption in their socialization period (up to six weeks or more) and may have been disturbed by the change in environments. Some common behavioural problems seen in cats, such as spraying in the home or even aggression, sometimes stem from socialization disruption, and the pet shop environment is not ideal or healthy for developing kittens. Thus, many of the larger, more responsible pet stores will not sell kittens for these reasons.

Rescued and re-homed cats

Most rescue centres usually have a wide range of cats available, both in age and type, from 'moggies' to pedigree cats. Frequently, moggies can be seen advertised in local newspapers or shop windows, or may even be offered by a family that has experienced an accidental pregnancy with their pet cat. These 'moggies' are always much cheaper than pedigree cats and are sometimes 'free to good homes'.

Cross-breeds of cats may be available at rescue centres, and specific breed rescue groups may even be available in your area. There are colour variations within breeds, ranging from white to lilac to black. Coat markings vary from self (one solid colour throughout the body) to tabby (striped) or spotted.

Your local area will often be home to individual cat lovers who take it upon themselves to rescue and re-home any cats and kittens that have been abandoned or whose keepers cannot care for them. A donation towards the 'home rescue' centre will usually suffice, although they will always welcome gifts of cat food and pet accessories.

must know

Organizations
All charitable cat rescue organizations require loving homes for the thousands of abandoned cats they receive each year. The staff involved with rehousing the cats should have a good idea of the temperament of each cat in their care. Tell them what you want and they can match your needs to one of their cats. Kittens from feral matings (involving a semi-wild cat) can be very instinctive and may always be shy and nervous around people.

If you are buying a rescue cat, don't go by appearances. Many cats are the unfortunate victims of circumstance and can be integrated into families to make affectionate, loyal companions.

Kitten or adult?

You must decide whether you want to get a kitten or an adult cat. You will need to choose which would be best suited to you and your family's lifestyle. There are some important questions to ask at this stage, so answer them realistically. The answers will be helpful when deciding which is the ideal cat for you.

must know

Choosing a kitten
If you decide to opt for a kitten, remember that it will take up a lot of your time as it will require several meals a day while it is young and will need periods of play and supervision. You cannot take it home and then expect it to fend for itself. You will also have to provide bedding and toys to keep the kitten comfortable and amused.

Young kittens

Healthy kittens are naturally playful, inquisitive and lively. However, they need a lot of attention in their early months. They must be fed small meals three or four times a day, as their stomachs are quite small and when they are growing fast they require lots of nourishment. All kittens need to be inoculated against common infections, so bear in mind that there will be veterinary bills. If you are a responsible cat keeper, it will be necessary to have your cat neutered, from about six to twelve months, to avoid any unwanted pregnancies in a female or to prevent a male cat from spraying (marking with urine).

Growing cats

In contrast to a kitten, a young adult cat will require less frequent meals and will not necessarily demand continual contact from its human companions. Mature cats will normally be toilet trained and are almost always more streetwise than kittens when it comes to the outside world beyond your home. However, kittens can usually be trained to use a litter tray as their indoor toilet. A properly socialized kitten will have been trained by its mother to urinate and defecate beyond the nesting site.

Older cats

At six months of age, cats do not require quite the same attention as young kittens. They need only two or, possibly, three meals a day. Cats become fully mature when they are about one year old.

Most adult cats are usually house trained and accustomed to living in a home environment. They can make the best house cats for elderly people because older felines are happy to lounge around. Indoor cats appear to thrive when they are kept in pairs, and some rescue centres have older cats they want to keep together. Provided their new home is warm and friendly, most mature cats will take very little time to settle down. However, despite all the precautions you take, some adult cats will still be unsettled by being transferred from an 'institutional' environment to your comfortable home. You should provide covered indoor litter trays to enable your cat to 'mark' and settle into its new territory.

All kittens are very inquisitive and love to explore. Any new object will be treated with interest and curiosity.

One or more cats?

Cats enjoy human companionship – being fed and groomed on a daily basis is a feline's idea of heaven. If your family's lifestyle means that everyone is out at work or school during the day, then it is probably wise to consider choosing to keep two cats.

Owning two cats

Two cats can play and interact with each other rather than getting bored with their own company and turning to other more destructive outlets for activity, such as damaging the furniture. If this is best for you, it is easier to introduce kittens of a similar age into your home at the same time. Two littermates are easiest, but it is possible to introduce kittens of a similar age from different breeders or sources with relative ease.

For a stress-free multi-cat household it is best to introduce your pets as kittens.

Introducing adult cats

Introducing two adult cats at the same time, unless they have been housed together, can be difficult because mature cats are more likely to display territorial aggression than kittens. Socializing adults is rarely accomplished without behavioural problems, which may not only include aggression towards each other but also indoor marking (spraying), scratching furniture and indoor urination and defecation. Unless you are familiar with keeping cats and you enjoy a 'challenge', do not consider purchasing two adult cats to keep in your home.

Male or female?

All cats, regardless of whether they are male or female, can make good pets. It is important to be a responsible cat owner and avoid unplanned pregnancies. To safeguard against an unwanted litter, it will be necessary, as your cat reaches sexual maturity, to arrange for it to be neutered.

Benefits of neutering

Mature cats that are not neutered can also be quite unpopular in a home environment. Males (toms) tend to mark their territory by spraying urine, both outside and inside the house and this behaviour attracts females. Males are more likely to wander off looking for a mate. Female cats (queens) come into 'season' periodically, and they are more likely to become restless. Females in 'season' frequently make loud caterwauling noises, especially if they have visual contact with other cats. They may also become very attached to their owners and require extra attention.

must know

Neutering costs
A kitten can be neutered at six months. It costs less for neutering males than females who will need more surgery. Most rescue cats will have been neutered.

Kittens socialize easily as they are less competitive than adult cats.

Health checks

It is important to make sure that you acquire a healthy kitten or cat. A kitten that develops infections in the early stages of its life can become disturbed and nervous later on in adulthood. Young kittens are particularly susceptible to infections when their immune systems are still being established.

Check the kitten's underside for any signs of knotted or wet fur.

Quick health check

When selecting your kitten (or adult cat), carefully and deliberately check that the coat is smooth and clean. The fur, especially on its underside, should not be knotted or wet. Closely inspect the coat for any signs of fleas (bites) or skin infections (bald or reddened skin patches). Watch the kitten and look out for any excessive scratching which could indicate the presence of parasites or infections.

A kitten's eyes should always be clean and bright and the third eyelid should not be visible. Any excess moisture or matting of the fur around the eyes could indicate an eye infection.

The kitten's (or cat's) anal region should also be clean and unsoiled. Gently feel under the abdomen which should be slightly rounded. Watch carefully to see whether the kitten walks properly and is not showing any signs of lameness.

Ears, nose and mouth

The ears should be clean inside and out. The mouth should be pink. Confirm that the teeth are clean and unbroken and that the gums are not inflamed by gently opening the kitten's mouth and inspecting the top and bottom of the inner jaws.

A kitten's nose should always be clean and moist. Any dryness or marks may indicate an infection. If you have any doubts about your kitten's health, arrange for an early health check from a veterinary surgeon or a senior animal nurse.

If there are several kittens to choose from, identify the one that seems outgoing and is in the centre of the litter activity. It's not wise to select a kitten that is sulking in the corner away from its siblings. Do not choose a sleeping kitten unless all the litter are sleepy and bundled up together and you have had the opportunity to watch them being active.

1 Run your hand over the body. The coat should be silky smooth.

2 Check the anal region; it should be clean and unsoiled.

3 The gums should be pink and the teeth should be clean.

4 Check that the eyes are bright and free from discharge.

Selecting the right kitten

It is a myth that someone with an animal behaviour background can take a snapshot observation of a litter of kittens or an older cat and then make the correct decision to avoid the nervous individual, decline the real extrovert and select the feline average. As we shall see, this well-meaning advice is not always realistic.

Making the right decision

Without the necessary information, it is difficult to time your visit to coincide with the best likelihood of activity from the kittens. However, the breeder may be able to predict the active times and suggest an optimum period for you. To make an accurate decision, based on the personality of a particular kitten, an observer would have to spend several hours, over many days, gaining an insight into their behaviour beyond those obvious forms that occur at sleep time and activity time.

When judging the 'group personality' of the litter, the best indicators come from prolonged contact with the mother. If she is calm and approachable, once you have entered the home and settled, and if she is sociable towards your non-intrusive handling, then it is likely that her kittens will show the same sociable personality. After observing the mother, it is advisable to make a couple of visits to check out the litter and select the kitten that shines out from the rest as being lively, inquisitive and healthy.

Kittens that have been well cared for and handled correctly will display natural curiosity and playfulness. In such a litter, your preference for shape and colour will probably override any other factors for selection.

The most realistic approach would be to choose an 'average' kitten in activity and personality. There is a very simple method of selecting a kitten – just hold out your hand. Sometimes it may appear as though a kitten will choose you!

Selecting the ideal kitten means both watching and handling individuals. One kitten will shine out from the rest of the litter.

Introverts and extroverts

Realistically, few people have the willpower to resist a group of soft and beautiful kittens, and, more often than not, a selection will be made on the spot. In this instance, if you want to own a playful kitten, then try to choose the extrovert 'explorer' over the timid introvert. This kitten is brave and wants to investigate the world beyond the nesting site. It will try to get out of your hands and escape into the excitement of the unknown, which may simply be represented by the room you are in. If you happen to be looking for the 'adventurer' in a kitten, then this one would be perfect for a busy family with children and an active lifestyle.

Questions to ask yourself when selecting a kitten or cat

Primary factor questions

Do you want a kitten or adult cat? Kittens will require more attention than adult cats as well as more frequent feeding. They are also more adaptable than adult cats. Kittens may explore without care and attention in dangerous situations, unlike an adult cat which will usually have learned, through bitter experience, to avoid dangers.

Mature individuals are often difficult to socialize because of the territorial nature of cats. More than one kitten can be socialized at the same time which means that they will interact with each other during daytime hours when most adults and young non-infant children are away from home.

Do you want a male or a female cat? Male cats (toms) may spray urine, both outside and inside the house, to mark territory and to attract females. Males tend to explore over larger territories looking for females. They are also more likely to go missing for long periods as they attempt to 'urine mark' in order to maintain a territory.

Female cats (queens) come into season periodically and may become restless day and night. Cats in season may be extremely vocal and can make long and loud noises especially towards other cats. They may become attached to a keeper and require extra attention. Neutering can prevent this.

Do you want a small or a large cat? This is not really a consideration when choosing a cat as there is only a slight difference in all domesticated breed sizes. British cats can grow large by cat standards. However, individuals of many cat breeds can grow large.

Do you want a shorthair or a longhair? Shorthaired breeds include British Shorthairs, Burmese, Siamese and Abyssinians but they can also be of Persian origin, such as the Exotic. They are easier to groom than longhairs, produce less hair and may be accommodated by people with slight allergies.

Longhaired breeds tend to be Orientals (angoras), Persians, Birmans, Turkish and Maine Coons but can also be seen in the common moggie. Longhaired cats produce more loose hairs, require regular grooming (at least three or four times a week) and may cause acute health problems for any family members with allergies. You must be prepared to groom such breeds regularly, preferably on a daily basis, to prevent their coat matting and reduce loose hairs.

Note: A dark-haired cat is more likely to trigger allergic symptoms in people with allergies than a light-haired cat.

Questions to ask yourself when selecting a kitten or cat

Secondary factor questions

Do you have a cat already?

If you are already keeping an adult cat it is usually simpler to introduce a new kitten into the household than a mature individual. Adult cats, when first introduced, may fight; they may also begin scratching and marking (spraying) furniture with urine.

An adult cat may initially object to the presence of a kitten, but careful socialization (introduction during daytime resting periods in a neutral room with 'controlled' handling) should prevent aggression. Always have a play pen or a cat carrying box available to restrict the movements of the kitten or an aggressive cat.

What home and lifestyle do you have?

A small to medium urban home with a modest garden or yard inhabited by family members sharing a busy lifestyle can be suitable for an outgoing cat or kitten. Although a number of cats with access to the outside environment can be socialized together, some competition is likely between growing cats if they are living in a reduced space.

A small to large rural home with an enclosed garden and a family that has a quieter lifestyle may be ideal for both longhaired and shorthaired cats or kittens. A shorthaired cat may suit families with little spare time to spend on grooming. A longhaired cat will require regular grooming every day.

Cat runs can be installed to restrict the movements of a house cat, yet allow access to an outside environment. They are ideal if you have a valuable pedigree cat and you don't want him to roam freely outside. They are also good for socializing more than one kitten in spacious conditions.

Where do you live?

Urban: In an urban location, your cat is more likely to encounter other cats once he has access to your garden or the surrounding area. This means he has a higher risk of infection and potential aggression. He is also more likely to be exposed to continual traffic flow and the dangers from road vehicles. Urban cats can 'learn' to be wary of traffic because of continual exposure.

Rural: In a rural location it is less likely that a cat with outside access could come into contact with feral cats. Thus the risks of cross-infection from exposure to other cats are diminished. Note that feral cats are usually nervous of human activity and they can be aggressive towards house cats. There is usually less traffic in a rural than an urban area, but rural cats can be naïve about fast-moving vehicles and are more susceptible to road traffic.

Adult cats

If you want to re-home an adult cat, try to avoid taking on a nervous or an aggressive one by visiting the rescue centre several times and offering the cats physical contact.

Assessing a cat

In rescue centres, the cats rarely show their true behaviours (beyond aggression and timidity) when kept in temporary accommodation. However, the staff may be able to give you a general assessment, which offers some pointers to a cat's sociability.

If a cat can be handled (stroked and picked up), that is an indicator of sociability. Nervous cats look for bolt-holes in the smallest places and should not be judged simply on a need to find sanctuary from a 'hostile world'. Such cats may stabilize eventually in a caring home and start being sociable. Prolonged observations and contact with a potential adoptee provides a more realistic assessment of personality.

If you already have a cat, then check with the breeder or rescue centre that an adult cat you may wish to acquire does not display aggressive or dominant behaviour towards other cats.

House cat or free-roaming cat?

The type of facilities you have and the access you offer to the outdoor environment will determine whether you get a pedigree or a moggie. Pedigree kittens, if they are socialized and possess good temperaments, will make great house cats. To prevent exposure to infections from outdoor cats and the dangers of roads, they are often restricted to the house and supervised while exercising within the garden, which should be enclosed securely. If you want your cat to roam freely outside, a moggie is a better choice.

Many house cats love looking out of the window and watching the world go by outside their home.

Risks to free-roaming cats

Cats that are unfamiliar with busy roads can find themselves 'frozen in headlights' and struck by vehicles – most feline fatalities are the result of night-time road traffic accidents. Other fatalities result from serious infections, such as 'cat flu' and cat leukaemia, which may be passed on by free-roaming cats. Poisons, which are laid down to kill unwanted pests and vermin, are another of the potential hazards for free-roaming cats.

Which is the better option?

Although some people believe that it is cruel to keep a house cat inside permanently, pedigree cats that have been born and raised indoors appear to be quite happy and contented to live within the protection and the comfort of their owners' homes. And with the increased number of motor vehicles on the roads today, an indoor cat is much safer and more likely to live a longer, healthier life than the outdoor 'free-roaming' pet.

must know

Feral cats
These cats live a wild existence and usually only tolerate human company, if at all, to access food. They hide away from people and are difficult to socialize and domesticate. If you are a novice or average cat owner rather than an expert, you should not entertain the idea of owning a feral cat.

Cats can find you

There are many cats who have 'wanderlust' and kitten litters that do not 'belong' to a particular keeper. Instead, they happily adopt several families within their local neighbourhood, who offer food and sometimes a safe, warm place to sleep at night.

Adopting a cat

The first you know of a cat adopting your family may occur when you find it sitting outside your front or back door. Such cats are often quite vocal, and there is a particular type of cry that can suggest starvation to most sympathetic people. Adopting these cats can be a gradual, surreptitious process that goes almost unnoticed until the realization finally dawns that your feline friend has decided to live at your home and has adopted you!

What to do

If a cat decides to turn up on your doorstep and wants to come and live with you, it may be worth checking locally to ascertain if anyone has reported a cat missing. You can make inquiries at the local veterinary clinics and look on shop notice boards. It is possible that someone has just moved into or left your area and your new-found friend has simply become confused.

Wandering cats may stay in the short term and then, as suddenly as they arrived, they may disappear. Always ensure that any new cat that arrives in this way is examined by your local veterinary surgeon for any signs of infections and ask about possible vaccinations.

Opposite: You are more likely to be 'adopted' by a moggie than a pedigree, such as this Siamese.

want to know more?

• To find out more about kittens for sale, look in your local newspaper or specialist cat magazines.
• To get a rescue cat, contact Cats Protection and visit one of their rescue centres. Email: cpl@cats.org.uk
• Alternatively phone Wood Green Animal Shelters: 01763 838329

weblinks

• Check out the Cat Protection website: www.cats.org.uk

2 The perfect kitten

Bringing your new kitten home can be slightly nerve-wracking for both of you. However, with a little care and attention, from the moment you pick him up until you introduce him into your home, you can start your relationship successfully. Your kitten will not know why he has been removed from his litter siblings and mother, but he will soon learn that a big, new world lies beyond his former home. Everything will be unfamiliar and strange to him, and it is up to you to settle him into his new home and reassure him that he is in safe hands.

Collecting your kitten

There cannot be many aspects of pet-keeping that are more exciting than bringing home your chosen companion. To ensure that this is a successful and stress-free occasion for everyone concerned, make a list in advance of all the items you require and devise a strategy for the family to follow.

Planning for the arrival

When bringing a kitten home for the first time or transporting him to the veterinary centre or cattery, it is important to keep him secure. There are many kinds of pet carriers and travel crates. Some are temporary boxes which are made out of cardboard, and these are suitable for short-term use and for emergencies, whereas others are made from hard-wearing plastic or plastic-coated wire and are ideal for long-term regular use.

Heading home

When collecting your kitten, be sure to place a clean towel, some kitchen roll or sheets of newspaper in the bottom of the carrier to soak up any accidents that may occur. Pick up the kitten gently but firmly, supporting his bottom with one hand, and place him in the carrier. Close the door quickly and then secure the fastener. Carry the box on your knees and ask the driver to drive smoothly without excessive braking or cornering to prevent sudden movements as you make your journey home.

Do not leave the kitten unattended when he is inside the carrier. When transporting him, take care that he cannot become over-heated or too cold.

must know

Plan ahead
Before collecting your kitten, get organized. You will need:
• A transport unit (crate or carrier) or temporary carrying box
• Kitchen roll, newspaper or an old towel to line the bottom of the box or crate in case of mishaps
• A notebook to list your kitten's existing diet and any recommendations made by the breeder or rescue centre
• A friend to drive the car for you, or to carry the cat box or crate

Opposite: Your kitten will soon settle in to his new home and in no time at all he will become a much-loved family member.

Settling in

When you arrive home, take the box and kitten into the room you have chosen for his first night. Close any doors that may offer a frightened kitten an opportunity to take flight. A little care at this early stage can prevent a great deal of heartache.

must know

Going outside
As your kitten gets to know you and you are confident that he will come when you call him, under your supervision he may make his first excursions to other parts of the house and eventually the garden.

Introducing your family

To help your new feline friend settle into your home quickly and become a much-loved member of the family, do not try to expose him to everyone at once. It is not necessary to introduce all the family members and any pets you may own to your new kitten on his first day.

Territorial security

Ideally, in the initial twenty-four hours, the kitten should be allowed to explore one room, which should be made secure from other animals. You must provide water, a small amount of food, a litter tray (a covered one in the case of an older kitten) and, most importantly, peace and quiet.

If you have adopted an older kitten or an adult cat, then it may well be advisable to ask the rescue centre for a small amount of his soiled litter. This 'waste' can be transferred to the new tray in your home, and this will ensure that your kitten will 'associate' faster with his new surroundings – through scent – and will often stimulate almost immediate usage of the tray. The additional benefit of this strategy is that it will also encourage an aspect of 'feline territorial security' which 'marking' either with urine or with faeces stimulates.

Handling your kitten

There is always a great temptation to keep picking up your new kitten. However, although it is very important to have positive physical contact with your pet, this should be done confidently and correctly if your relationship is to develop with trust.

Calm and supervision

Try to resist the temptation to pick up your kitten at every available opportunity. Sometimes it is better just to watch him explore his new surroundings or allow him to curl up in a quiet place for a cat nap.

It is important that infants and small children should always be supervised during any new cat or kitten encounters. This will prevent the possibility of any rough handling and accidental aggression or undue attention by either party.

Lifting a kitten

While your kitten will be fairly easy to scoop up, it is important that you support his bottom with one hand while holding his body gently and firmly with the other. Hold him close to you if you have to carry him anywhere. A cuddle while you are sitting down and relaxing in a chair may even turn into a cat nap. However, on other occasions, your kitten may want to play (chew and scratch, climb and jump) and you must be careful not to drop him from a standing height. Make your contact positive by being brief and offering firm but gentle strokes. You may want to dangle a piece of wool after placing him back on the ground, or offer a small food treat as an extra reward for good contact.

To pick up your kitten, gently slip your hand under his tummy (top). Gripping gently but firmly, scoop him up with your other hand (above) positioned firmly under his bottom for support.

Introducing other pets

If you already have a dog or another cat, introducing them to a new arrival should always be controlled and strictly under your supervision to avoid any accidents or aggressive behaviour.

Many dogs and cats can learn to live quite happily together.

Introducing a dog

If your dog is friendly towards cats, you can play a 'click and treat' retrieval game with him whilst the newcomer is exploring in the same room. A 'clicker' is a thumb-sized unit that can be used over a period of time to signal that a food treat is to be given. This device can be used to promote good behaviour, such as sitting and recall. Use distraction if your dog becomes boisterous. If he shows aggression, then use a reward, such as a food treat or game with his favourite toy, to draw him away from the kitten and then separate them for the time being until you can initiate a socialization programme.

Dealing with aggressive behaviour

If your dog acts aggressively towards your new kitten, it is important not to make any events 'exciting' by giving them your attention; this may have the undesired effect of reinforcing the dog's behaviour. Use special training discs to signal non-reward and end-behaviour rather than shout at your dog. These are small brass discs on a cord that can be shown to the dog at the same time a food treat is removed. After using them for a while, they will automatically signal to your dog that a reward will be removed. This is usually enough to encourage him to stop any antisocial behaviour.

Rewarding good friends

Reward your dog with special treats if he behaves well around the kitten. If you aren't confident that you can control his aggression, muzzle him when trying to socialize him with the kitten. Do not keep them separated permanently in the home; there will come a time when they will be brought together accidentally with potential aggression. 'Controlled socialization', with food rewards to both parties for good behaviour, should be undertaken. Note that the same rules and techniques apply if you are introducing an adult cat to a dog or resident pet.

Smaller pets

If you also keep small pets, such as mice, gerbils, hamsters, guinea pigs and rabbits, they must be securely housed so your kitten cannot gain access to them. Cats are natural hunters and may regard these animals as legitimate prey. However, some can learn to live together.

Cats can live in harmony with other small pets, such as rabbits and guinea pigs, which they would normally regard as prey.

Indoor safety

Kittens are naturally inquisitive creatures, and they are likely to explore every nook and cranny of their new home, so it is very important to make your home 'cat safe'. Making a home safe for a kitten or cat is similar to taking safety precautions for a child.

must know

Safe collars
Even basic collars can be dangerous for kittens if they are loose fitting. Kittens can easily become hooked up on things and trapped, and the results can be fatal. The Cats Protection recommend a special circlet collar which is extremely safe.

Household chemicals

If there is a possibility of your kitten coming into direct contact with detergents and other dangerous household cleaning solutions, then the potential for a fatality exists. Although a cat is unlikely to lick up a solution, he could easily knock over a bottle and walk through the spilt liquid. The chemical on his paws could irritate his sensitive skin or, even worse, be digested when he attempts to clean himself.

Electric cables

Any exposed electric cables are another potential hazard for a playful kitten. Make sure they are not frayed because if your kitten begins to play with an unsafe lead he can easily be electrocuted. Take care that no long leads are hanging down from electric kettles and any other electrical appliances.

Windows

It is also very important that all windows are secure and they can be shut or locked unless your cat has safe access through a ground-floor window to the outside. There is always the possibility that a kitten could escape through an open window on an upper floor or even over a balcony and could sustain a serious injury in such a fall.

Sharp implements

It is vital that sharp implements, such as knives, drawing pins and needles, are kept safely out of reach of your kitten. Most of these kitchen items should be stored safely away in drawers or hung up on hooks on the wall.

Fireplaces

Fireplaces provide access to chimneys, and these entrances can become traps for inquisitive kittens. Block them off for the first six to twelve months.

Hidden dangers indoors

Some dangers may not be immediately apparent. Hot baths could prove not only difficult for a kitten to climb out of but could be fatal should he fall into

Windows that are left open can be dangerous for adult cats and kittens, especially if you own a house cat or if the open window is on an upper storey.

Kittens will seek refuge in all sorts of nooks and crannies, and nervous individuals may start chewing on wires or live electric cables. Take care!

A kitten's natural curiosity can sometimes get him into trouble. Make sure any chemicals, even diluted in water, and other toxic substances are kept securely sealed and out of reach.

the water accidentally. Open doors offer access to the outside world to an inquisitive kitten. If yours is to be an 'indoor cat', it is essential to close the front and back doors carefully on every occasion you enter or leave the house. It is also important to shut other less obvious doors inside your home.

Traps for the unwary

It is advisable not to leave the washing machine door open (or any other household appliances that could imprison a kitten) as he could easily explore inside when you are unaware or distracted. It is also sensible to keep wardrobe and cupboard doors closed to prevent him from accidentally becoming trapped inside. It may surprise pet owners to know that rubbish bins can also be a potential hazard to a young and curious kitten. If he can gain access to the contents of a waste bin, he may encounter a wide range of dangerously sharp items, such as open cans, which could easily cause nasty cuts.

There are many other dangers to a small kitten in the home, ranging from an open fire (always use a fire guard) to a simple curtain sash cord (make sure that it is not accessible to your kitten). Whilst it is impossible to foresee every danger in your home, it is always wise to try and reduce any potentially risky opportunities that exist for a young cat.

House plants

You should also be aware that some house plants are potentially dangerous to a kitten. Many cats and kittens like to play with plants and chew them. Among the common plants that are potentially toxic are Fuchsia, Ivy, Poinsettia and Philodendron.

Outdoor safety

Once your kitten has been vaccinated and you are sure he knows his way around the house, you can start introducing him gradually to the outdoors. Ensure that you are there to supervise at first and that you pay attention to certain outdoor safety aspects.

Poisonous plants and substances

Some garden plants, such as Azalea, Sweet Pea, Rhododendron and Clematis, are poisonous to cats. Although a cat is unlikely to eat them, it is advisable not to stock your garden too heavily with these plants. Observe your kitten closely when you let him out into the garden to ensure he does not come into contact with them. Be aware also that some trees, such as the yellow-flowering Laburnum, produce poisonous seeds, and these should be avoided or access to them should be restricted.

To avoid distressing accidents, always ensure that any toxic substances, such as pesticides, together with sharp gardening equipment, are safely locked away in a garden shed.

Garden ponds

These are potential disaster areas for kittens. They should not have steep sides which would make it difficult for a kitten to climb out if he accidentally fell into the water. Place a net over the water or install a low fence around the pond to prevent access to cats. Formal ponds can be shielded with a netted frame. By taking a few simple precautions in your garden, you can prevent potential accidents and your cat should live a long and happy life with you.

This Norwegian Forest Cat is surveying the world from up a tree. Although they rarely get stuck, cats can sometimes climb too high and may need rescuing.

Scratching posts

It is normal, healthy behaviour for all cats and kittens to scratch. This enables them not only to mark via glands in their paws but also may help to keep their claws in tip-top condition. If you do not provide your pet with a scratching post, he will probably use the furniture as an alternative.

This mini activity centre doubles as an attractive scratching post.

Using a scratching post

Kittens learn best by example, and to encourage your kitten to scratch on a post, rather than on your best furniture, you must gently place his front paws on the post until the idea is accepted. Be patient and keep doing this – a healthy kitten will soon get the message and will start using the post. Note that when you are training an adult cat to use a scratching post, then it is best to place it in a really prominent position where the cat has shown an inclination to stand, stretch and open up his claws.

Start scratching

During the early training of young cats and kittens, it is always a good idea to keep the scratching post in the same place. However, if you find that there is one particular piece of furniture that your kitten likes to scratch, then it could be worthwhile to position the scratching post in front of it.

If your kitten is very active and you observe him scratching on the furniture, it is best to interrupt his behaviour with a reward signal (a bell or clicker sound that has become linked to a food treat) and then gently carry him to the scratching post, placing his front paws on the upright.

Types of posts

A great variety of scratching posts are now available from pet shops. Some posts are an integral part of interesting platforms or raised beds. Scratching posts can be scented with catnip and can become a place where cat treats can be left in order to encourage your cat to approach and use them.

Scratching posts can be quite elaborate and can incorporate climbing stations and high platforms. They provide hours of stimulating entertainment for an indoor kitten or adult cat.

Using a litter tray

Cats and kittens should have access to outdoors (through a cat flap) or to a litter tray at all times. Litter trays are indoor toilets for cats, and they are usually made from moulded plastic and are available in various designs and sizes from pet stores.

must know

Punishment
Never smack or hit a cat in response to problem behaviours. If he does something that is not allowed, a sharp tone of voice and the word 'No!' are usually sufficient. If this fails, clap your hands loudly. For more obstinate cats, a quick squirt of water from a plant spray or water pistol may be necessary. This method is very effective in curing a cat from walking on kitchen surfaces where food is to be prepared.

Hygiene

The litter trays that are designed with hoods are probably the most hygienic to use, as any smells are contained and will not penetrate the room, and the litter material is prevented from spilling out. Covered litter trays will also offer the cat or kitten a degree of privacy when going to the toilet.

The litter tray is an essential item for all indoor cats and kittens and those who are confined to the house during the day or evening. However, in order to maintain the health of your cat or kitten, it is essential that you clean out the tray on a daily or, at least, on a regular basis.

Training your kitten

It should be relatively easy to train your new kitten to use a litter tray as he will probably have used one already in the breeder's home. Indeed, kittens will usually have observed their mother using a litter tray and will learn by her example.

For the first few days after you bring your new kitten home, you should regularly place him in the tray. Position the tray where it is easily accessible and always keep it in the same place. A new kitten will quickly learn where the litter tray is situated and will become toilet-trained.

Toileting problems

If your kitten or cat begins toileting or spraying (marking) in your home following the successful use of a litter tray, he may have developed a behaviour that needs treatment (see page 90).

Going to the toilet is not simply about urinating and defecating. Cats leave scent signals, or messages, which are intended to offer marker information to other cats. These messages include information about territory boundaries, sex, oestrus cycles, testosterone and oestrogen levels and, possibly, dominance. Fresh foreign scents made by cats and other animals within your cat's territory can cause alarm whereas old scents can be ignored and over-marked with the cat's own scent.

Kittens learn by example, and they will watch their mother using the litter tray.

Insecure kittens

In cases of insecurity (marking within the house), reduce your kitten's territory within your home by restricting him to one room – ideally, one with a cat flap exit to the outside world. Kittens and cats who are confident should have the run of your house. If the kitten refuses to use the litter tray provided it is probably due to insecurity or, in adult cats, it can sometimes be linked to an earlier bad experience. To combat this problem, you can offer extra litter trays in different locations throughout the house. Covered litter trays can offer a nervous cat an element of secrecy, and clumping litter has been found to be more attractive to most cats in this situation.

Even young kittens can learn to use a litter tray and will become toilet-trained. Make sure that you change the litter regularly.

Using a cat flap

If your kitten can roam freely outside, it is advisable to fit a door cat-flap to give him the freedom to come and go as he pleases. There are many different flaps but it is important that the one you choose is not positioned too high or too low for a kitten.

must know

Perspex or solid?
Perspex flaps through which a cat can see the outside world are easier to introduce than solid flaps. However, they also enable other cats to look in, which some nervous felines may find disconcerting. Both flap types can be locked securely but cats may try to open the locked perspex types and get frustrated when they cannot pass through.

Making the cat flap safe

Kittens are quick to understand how to use a cat flap. Just encourage them to pass through gently a few times and they will soon learn what to do.

Magnetized or key-collar coded cat flaps are the best sort to install because they will permit only your kitten – rather than neighbourhood moggies – to exit and enter through the flap. This feature can be paramount for insecure kittens and young cats who may find competition with other outdoor cats, especially those exhibiting territorial aggression, rather frightening. The nervousness that can follow these stressful incidents can encourage a young cat to mark, or spray, indoors.

Indoor cats

Cat flaps for indoor cats can be installed to create a connection between your home and a secure outdoor run in the garden. Kittens who are allowed access to an outdoor run will benefit from the safety that comes of living indoors while still experiencing the diversity of outdoor life. Ideally, cat runs should be as large as possible and fitted with different platform shelves, which are placed at varying heights. You can also position a tree stump or a post in the run for the kitten to use for scratching. A suitable waterproof shelter should also be provided in case it starts to rain.

Exercising your kitten

All kittens need exercise. However, the amount they require will depend on the breed, as some felines are more exuberant than others. Like adult cats, kittens love to climb and their strong hind legs are excellent for jumping. If your kitten is allowed outdoors, there is no doubt that he will enjoy climbing trees.

Outdoor kittens

Sitting on walls, fences and other elevations gives your kitten or young cat the ideal vantage point to watch over his territory. Being high up, he will also be more successful at spotting potential dangers, such as other cats or dogs. To maintain his territory, he will have to patrol and scent his boundaries regularly. Most outdoor cats get sufficient exercise from this to keep them fit and healthy.

Indoor kittens

Kittens who are kept indoors can become lethargic and bored. If your kitten is a house cat, it might be a good idea to have two cats as they will provide each other with essential animal contact and play. Kittens who are the best of friends will enjoy chasing each other around the house. They will also benefit from scratching posts (see pages 42–43). Platforms are useful as they enable a kitten to climb and sit in an elevated position as he would outside.

Suitable toys

It is necessary to provide the indoor kitten with a varied selection of toys. There are many elaborate toys on the market, but large cardboard boxes are

Owning two indoor cats can help prevent boredom and behavioural problems. They will amuse each other and enjoy playing together.

Nearly all cats love to climb, and outdoor ones will enjoy shinning up trees and watching the world from a high vantage point.

All sorts of unlikely objects can become amusing toys for kittens, like this unprepossessing foil ball.

cheap and are usually a successful way of keeping your pet entertained. Kittens love jumping, hiding and peeping into boxes. Small balls, with or without bells, are another favourite toy which they always enjoy playing with.

Absolutely anything bobbing about on the end of a string is an irresistible attraction for an inquisitive kitten. However, don't leave a kitten unsupervised to play with this type of toy. It has been known for them to become entangled in a long piece of string and even to strangle themselves in the process.

Track toys, where a ball is 'pawed' by the kitten around a circular track, have proved to be extremely successful during testing by animal behaviourists.

Home alone

Many kittens will sleep for long periods during the day. Leaving your kitten alone in the house while you are out at work should not create any major problems provided that he has the necessary food, water, litter tray and toys to keep him healthy and amused. It is acceptable to confine a kitten to one room, such as the kitchen, while you are away from home provided that you take the necessary safety precautions (see page 38).

Collars, harnesses and leads

If your kitten is to be allowed to roam freely out of doors, it is essential that he wears a collar and a tag containing your address or, better still, that he is micro-chipped. These methods enable you, the owner, to be traced if he gets lost and is later recovered. There are many types of collars on the market today, although in the UK Cats Protection provides the safest with its circlet type. Collars with bells are useful as they help you to hear if your kitten is nearby. Bells can also be beneficial in warning birds if your kitten is stalking them. Train him to wear a collar from as early an age as possible.

Sometimes it is possible to teach a kitten to walk on a lead, and some breeds, especially Burmese, are happier lead walking than others. It is also a good way to introduce the outside world to your kitten. If he regularly walks on a lead he will also need to wear a harness. If you decide to lead-train him, it is advisable for him to become accustomed to wearing a harness from an early age. Lead-training is a gradual process and you must be patient. Start by placing the harness on him for short periods while he is moving around the house. You must not try to 'walk' him at this stage. After a while, when he's used to the harness, try walking him around the garden. With time and patience, you should be successful.

Kitten health

Giving the correct diet, care and attention to your kitten is only one aspect of maintaining him in good health. You should take him to the local vet for his vaccinations and regular check-ups.

Make an appointment

When you acquire a new kitten it is advisable to register him with a local veterinary clinic, and make an appointment to see the vet as soon as possible for a full check-up and to discuss inoculations and a suitable worming regime. Your kitten can be given vaccines for protection against feline influenza, feline enteritis and feline chlamydial infection, either separately or in combination, from nine weeks of age onwards. If your kitten should ever become ill, it will help if your local veterinary clinic is already familiar with him and he is accustomed to going there and being handled by the staff.

What to look for

When you handle or groom your kitten, get him accustomed to being examined. Use these times together as an opportunity to check on his general state of health and to identify the tell-tale signs of any potential problems so that they can be treated quickly before they become more serious.

Coat and skin
The coat should be sleek and glossy with no bald patches. The skin should be free of fight wounds and scratches with no signs of parasites.

Anal region
This should be clean with no indications of soreness or diarrhoea.

Tail
The tail should be smooth and free from any scratches or wounds.

Eyes and nose
The eyes should be bright, clear and free from any discharge. The nose should be soft and damp with no signs of discharge.

Ears
The ears should be healthy and pink inside with no signs of discharge; not lots of dark wax.

Weight
A healthy cat should look right for his size – neither too fat nor too thin.

Mouth
The gums should be pink and free from inflammation. The teeth should be clean and unbroken. The breath should not smell unpleasant.

Paws
The paws should be clean with no tenderness or swelling.

Signs of ill health

By checking your kitten regularly, you can help prevent many common health problems. If you are ever in doubt about his health, ring the veterinary surgery and ask their advice.

Check the kitten's coat carefully for tell-tale signs of fleas. The droppings will look like fine black powder in the fur.

Make sure that the kitten's ears are pink and healthy with no signs of any discharge.

Symptoms to look for

Always examine your kitten regularly, and keep watch for any of the following symptoms:

• Prolonged sleeping, lethargy or hiding can be characteristics of an unhealthy kitten.

• Dietary changes, e.g. appetite loss or excessive drinking, can also indicate a health problem.

• Frequent vomiting, diarrhoea and/or blood in the faeces are always a cause for concern.

• A kitten can quickly become very dehydrated, and if this condition persists, you must seek the advice of your veterinary surgeon as quickly as possible.

• Frequent sneezing and/or coughing, and laboured breathing are signs that a kitten could possibly have a respiratory disorder.

• Weight loss, worms passed in the faeces and diarrhoea could indicate internal parasites. Your veterinary surgeon will be able to give you a suitable worming medication. To prevent worm infestations, it is advisable to worm your kitten regularly. Regular worming should begin at six weeks of age and continue every two to three months, increasing to once every three to four months for adult cats.

• If your kitten has difficulty when walking or is in pain, it is possible that he could have been involved in a road traffic accident and could be bleeding internally. Contact your vet immediately.

- Runny eyes could be a sign that your kitten has an eye infection. Your vet will be able to supply you with eye drops to treat this problem.
- Inflammation of the ears could mean that your kitten has an ear infection. Again, you should seek the advice of your veterinary surgeon.
- Excessive scratching or frantic licking could be a sign of fleas. Check the coat carefully for flea droppings, which look like fine black powder at the base of the fur. If you suspect them, seek out the advice of your vet as soon as possible for treatment. Buy a flea collar as a preventative measure.

Going to the veterinary clinic

In an ideal world, your kitten would make several car journeys before visiting the vet for the first time. All kittens and new cats require immunization and a general check-up, and this will necessitate travel, sometimes for only the second time in their lives.

Randomly crate your kitten or put him in a carrier before going to the vet. This will condition him to the carrier and should help prevent an unpleasant association being made. If he only goes in a carrying box for trips to the vet, he will learn to associate it with difficult rather than pleasant experiences.

Make the experience of visiting the vet swift and rewarding. Arrange an appointment for a quiet time if possible. Only take your kitten out of the carrier or crate when you are safely inside the examination room and the door has been closed securely behind you. Write down any queries you may have beforehand so that, hopefully, these can be dealt with speedily. Give your kitten a food treat when you return home afterwards.

Diet and feeding

Kittens, like all juvenile animals, require small, regular feeds as they have very tiny stomachs and can only digest modest amounts of food. They also display growth spurts and these need to be fuelled with food to prevent weight loss.

must know

Prey
Outdoor kittens will often bring prey, as a trophy or offering, into the home. Prey targets can range from small birds, rodents and insects to even juvenile rabbits. This instinctive hunting behaviour, which occurs even in well-fed kittens, can be extremely difficult to eradicate. Some kittens are natural hunters and thrive when they are stalking prey. A warning bell on the collar or a 'sonic unit' can not only alert potential prey but also reduce successful strike rates.

Types of food

A wide variety of food types are available for today's kitten. They range from canned and semi-moist foods to dry 'complete' products. The type of food to feed your kitten depends on his age (see page 56). Better-quality foods will inevitably cost more but will reflect a higher standard of contents and, in most cases, the considerable nutritional research that has been undertaken by the manufacturers. Each type of food has its benefits and disadvantages.
• Canned foods: Although these contain a great amount of moisture, some vitamins and minerals can be lost in the fluid.
• Dried foods: These have the advantage of being 'balanced' with a special formula for protein, amino acids, vitamins and minerals, but sometimes kittens find this type of food unappetizing.
• Semi-moist foods: These are popular with some kittens and their owners.

Note: There may be times, especially with queens (females), when your vet will recommend higher- or reduced-protein foods for your kitten. Always follow these recommendations because they are based on clinical research. Note that many of the larger cat food manufacturers do provide feeding guides.

Indoor and outdoor kittens

Another consideration when you are deciding on how much food to offer and the frequency of meals is whether you have an indoor or an outdoor kitten. The nutritional requirements of an active outdoor kitten would be slightly greater than those of a less active indoor kitten due to the amount of energy

Occasionally you may need to hand-rear a kitten. This four-week-old Singapura needs to be fed with a milk substitute through a syringe.

they expend. Bear in mind that all kittens will need some access to grass. They nibble grass to aid the regurgitation of fur, and thus they may benefit from being given small amounts in their diet. For indoor kittens or those who are given an outdoor run, it is possible to grow troughs of grass that can be rotated after use.

How much and how often?

Between four and six weeks, a kitten will need four to five feeds of moist food per day. This feeding regime should be followed up – from six weeks onwards – with a combination of solids, including

Kitten feeding guide

Under 3 weeks*	Consult a veterinary surgeon, breeder or a rescue centre expert for advice on feeding. The kitten would require a substitute for his mother's milk and may also need a vitamin and mineral supplement.
4–6 weeks	Feed 1 teaspoon, or slightly more, of liquid-consistency kitten food which has been mixed with some baby milk substitute 4–5 times per day.
6–12 weeks	Kittens should now be gradually weaned from moist food. Feed 2–3 teaspoons of solid kitten food (canned, moist and semi-moist or dried) 4–5 times per day.
3–6 months	Increase the amounts of solid foods, gradually scaling down from 5 times to 2–3 times per day.

* Kittens should not be removed from the litter at this age because any interruption to normal socialization can lead to nutritional deficiencies and behavioural problems later on in an adult cat.

fresh, canned or dried foods, although one feed can be a paste which is based on special cat milk and baby kitten food. By the time a kitten is eight weeks of age and ready to leave the litter and go to his new home, he should be eating solid foods.

The progressive weeks (months two to six) should see a gradual reduction in the number of feeds to two or three per day. The amount of food should be increased accordingly. See the table opposite for advice on which foods to give your kitten.

This ten-week-old Bengal kitten is eating his meal with relish. By this age, kittens should be fed solid foods.

want to know more?

• For advice on looking after a kitten, talk to your vet or contact the Feline Advisory Bureau. Tel: 01747 871872 Or email them on: information@fabcats.org
• For specialist books on kittens, see *RSPCA Pet Guide: Care for Your Kitten* (Collins) and Sarah Heath's *Cat and Kitten Behaviour* (Collins): www.harpercollins.co.uk

weblinks

• Free information on every aspect of caring for a kitten from The Blue Cross website: www.allaboutpets. org.uk
• You can buy cat litter and litter trays online: www.petplanet.co.uk

3 The adult cat

Care and consideration for your cat is much more than an expression of love or altruism; it is a rewarding investment bringing many tangible benefits both to the cat and you, his owner. Regular inspection, maintenance and simple preventive measures will ensure a longer, happier life for your pet. Veterinary bills will be significantly reduced, and the chances of cat to human transmission of ailments – always a minute possibility – diminishes.

Daily care

An important aspect of daily care and how you look after your cat will depend not only on his breed, coat type and whether he is kept indoors or allowed outdoors but also on his personality.

The feline personality

Different feline personalities will demand different attention levels. Independent, outgoing cats are 'outdoor' types and may only be around you when it suits them: at feeding, relaxation and sleeping times. An indoor house cat may follow you around, brushing up against your shins (marking and 'possessing' you) and calling out for food and your attention.

Active cats want more food than less active ones. They may also need more grooming because they are more likely to be 'out and about'. Their journeys through undergrowth, trees, along dusty footpaths and walls, hedgerows and fences will bring them into contact with cobwebs and dirt. A tangled coat can soon become matted if you don't give your cat a daily grooming session. Less active indoor cats need less food than their outdoor cousins and should require less grooming, too.

Shorthairs are easy to look after as they do not require much grooming. They make good outdoor cats.

must know

Reward and punishment
Never smack or shout at a cat for his apparent antisocial behaviour. This aggressive reaction will create more apprehension on the part of the cat and it could destroy any trust that may have developed between you and your pet. It is better to say 'No' to your cat, or to have a sound signal that you have already developed to show him an association with any problem behaviour and the removal of a food reward.

Shorthairs make the best outdoor cats as they have less coat to groom and less dirt to accumulate. Longhairs may be better suited to indoor life as they are less likely to encounter outdoor grime. However, some, like Norwegian Forest Cats, need the freedom to roam freely and do not settle well indoors.

The quiet cat

Kittens that suffer too many changes or difficulties during the first six weeks of life are often introverted and may be shy and non-sociable. They may be nervous around people and animals, and hide away from anyone or anything they perceive as a threat.

Rather than force yourself onto an introverted cat, gently draw him out of his nervousness. A quiet cat can be made to feel more secure by controlled handling (not too much fussing and stroking). Create positive interaction around feeding, play and grooming. If the cat is too clingy and gets too much attention, his nervousness will be reinforced and your absences would then have a greater impact.

The contrast between your presence (lots of fuss and attention) and your absence (no contact) can be too great for a nervous cat, so control your contact. A quiet cat is often contented with home life and may find the outside world too nerve-wracking.

The outgoing cat

The outgoing, or extroverted, kitten may also have experienced difficulties in early socialization. Instead of becoming withdrawn, this cat becomes outgoing and lively, aggressive and sometimes too demanding. He will often jump onto your knee as soon as you sit down. Groom or stroke him for a few minutes and then break off contact before any aggression (biting or scratching) can occur. He can feel more secure and be less demanding with controlled handling and positive interaction, created around feeding, play and grooming. These cats tend to be 'hunters' and make better outdoor pets than indoor ones.

Handling an adult cat

All physical contact with an adult cat must be based on confidence and firm handling on your part.

1 Start by encouraging the cat to climb onto your knee. A firm stroke and a food treat will make sure that this contact is very positive.

2 Once this has been repeated over a few days, it is time to pick up the cat from a floor position and carry him to a chair to offer him a cuddle. First, call the cat to you and tickle his chin or stroke his coat.

3 Crouch down and, supporting him under his bottom with one hand, use the other hand to cradle your pet to your chest. Don't stand up immediately, especially if there is any possibility that the cat will 'protest' (scratch and/or bite) about being handled.

4 If he struggles, put him down gently without dropping him – this is safer and easier to achieve from your crouched position. A badly-handled cat will immediately become wary of being picked up following a difficult encounter.

If you are not confident about handling an adult cat, then ask a member of your family or a friend who is used to picking up a cat to do so and to place the cat on your knee. Have a small food treat ready for him and stroke him firmly. Rewards and positive handling will ensure that the cat makes a good association with you, his owner.

When picking up a cat, be sure to support him under his bottom while cradling him to your chest.

Grooming your cat

Cats are continually licking their fur and their paws to keep themselves clean and in good condition. They will often groom each other (known as allogrooming), and social groups use this behaviour to promote good relationships.

must know

Grooming tools
You will need the following grooming tools to keep your cat's coat healthy. You can buy them in most pet stores.
• Fine or wide-toothed comb
• Soft and hard brushes
• Hand glove brushes
• Soft cloth or chamois
In addition, you may need these optional items of equipment:
• Claw clippers
• Bowl or baby bath of lukewarm water
• Cotton balls for cleaning

Establish a routine

You can help your cat in this task by establishing a grooming routine and ensuring that flea infestations, skin infections and knotted coats do not develop. Remember that when you groom him, you are also promoting your relationship and helping to confirm the bond between the two of you. Shorthaired cats are relatively easy to groom, especially if a twice-weekly session has already been established from kittenhood. However, longhaired cats will require daily grooming to prevent any tangling, knotting and problems with loose hairs.

Healthy coats

Regular grooming will prevent the build-up of loose hairs which can be ingested by your cat when he is self-grooming. The ingestion of too many hairs can result in fur balls developing in his stomach which, in turn, can lead to the regurgitation of hair and of food. In acute cases, the fur ball can lead to an obstruction in the bowel which would require urgent veterinary attention. By grooming your cat on a daily basis, there will also be less hairs on your clothing and furniture.

To rid your cat's coat of any loose hairs and also to maintain the coat in first-class condition, you should use the combination of a comb and a glove brush or soft brush. It is important to have the correct tools, so consider investing in the grooming accessories listed in the box opposite.

Ready, steady, groom!

Have your accessories ready in the early days and then wait for your cat to sit on your lap. Immediately your cat arrives for contact with you, begin gently brushing the coat. If your cat is nervous, offer a small food treat in order to turn the grooming experience into a 'positive event'. You may have to gently restrain him with your free non-grooming hand. Be prepared to be gentle but firm when you begin grooming your cat. Eventually, it is best to call him to you for a grooming session so that it occurs on your instruction rather than on his whim. Once the cat has accepted the basic concept of grooming, you can become more thorough in your technique.

Longhairs, such as this Persian, will need regular and intensive grooming to keep their coats really silky and free of tangles.

Shorthaired cats

1 Use a soft brush or glove brush to draw off any of the outer loose hairs from the cat's coat.
2 Take a fine-toothed comb and groom the back and head of your cat, initially combing the fur in the direction of the coat hairs.
3 Following this careful brushing and combing, change direction to comb against the fur, which will remove any deep-lying hairs that are loose.
4 Once the 'top grooming' has been achieved,

There are several types of glove brushes with varying degrees of 'grip' to strip loose hairs from a shorthaired or a longhaired cat. They also work well on fabrics, carpets and furniture.

turn the cat over. Support his head on your stomach and his bottom on your lap. Groom the underside in much the same way as his back and head.

5 Some owners finish a session by rubbing their cat's coat with a damp cloth (or even a chamois leather) to put a shine on the fur. A happy cat will often be in 'seventh heaven' by the time you finish this grooming exercise, and you should not be surprised if he complains at the end – he may not want you to stop.

Longhaired cats

Most longhaired cats will require grooming every day if their coats are to be kept free of loose hairs, tangles and matting. You will need more grooming tools than for a shorthaired cat – you must use a combination of soft and stiff brushes, wide- and fine-toothed combs and a hand glove or cloth.

Head and back

1 Brush your cat gently with a hand glove or a grooming brush. Follow the hair line on the back, softly brushing away from the head towards the tail. Repeat this procedure several times.

2 Brush in the opposite direction, from the tail to the head, loosening as much hair as possible.

3 If you encounter any knots, try to unravel them by hand or with a wide-toothed comb. If there is a stubborn knot of hair, which is rarely encountered if regular, daily grooming is undertaken, it may be necessary to carefully snip away the strands with a pair of round-tipped nail scissors.

4 Follow up with the stiff brush, repeating the whole procedure until the coat brushes easily.

Down under

Once the cat's head and back have been groomed, gently but firmly, turn your cat over and then repeat this grooming procedure on the underside until all of the coat has been teased, brushed and back-brushed. Not all cats are thrilled by this part of the grooming session – an indignant cat will often attempt a fast exit at this stage. So try to anticipate this and reassure your cat accordingly.

1 Gently brush the underside of your cat, teasing out any knots in the long fur by hand or carefully cutting them out with scissors.

2 Now follow this brushing stage with a thorough combing session, first combing with the hair along the lie and then back-combing it.

3 Use a hand glove brush at the end or a damp cloth, chamois or soft brush to 'polish' off the coat. Your cat should look fabulous with a soft, silky coat which is free of knots and tangles. The end result will make all your hard work and effort worthwhile. Afterwards, take time to examine your cat's ears, eyes, nose and mouth (see pages 70–71).

Grooming is a natural behaviour for a cat, but excessive grooming can lead to the development of fur balls in the cat's stomach.

must know

Flea check
Always check your combs and brushes by tapping and shaking them on to a white card. Look out for any odd specks that may reveal the tell-tale signs of a flea infestation. The early detection of fleas can make treatment much more effective.

Grooming a longhaired cat

Grooming is usually a daily requirement if you have a longhaired cat. Without a regular 'brushing and combing' session, your cat's coat will quickly become matted and knotted and it will be difficult to groom. A healthy cat will benefit greatly from 'care grooming' because this task can reduce the development of fur balls from ingested hair and also reduce the potential for parasite infestations.

While you are grooming, make sure that you check your cat's skin, ears, eyes, nose, paws and backside for any tell-tale signs of health problems. And after the grooming session, do remember to reward your cat for his patience and good behaviour by offering his favourite treat.

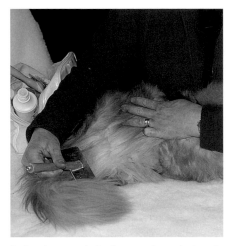

1 Carefully feel your way through the coat, using your fingers to gently unravel any loose knots and tangles you encounter.

2 Brush or comb the fur away from the head towards the tail, holding your cat firmly but gently and talking to him.

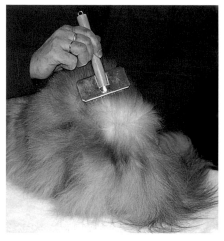

3 Comb or brush the fur in the opposite direction. Be gentle and do not drag the brush or comb through the cat's coat.

4 Gently brush the ruff around the cat's neck and the head. Remember to remove the collar if your cat wears one.

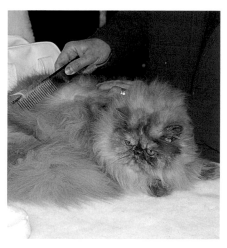

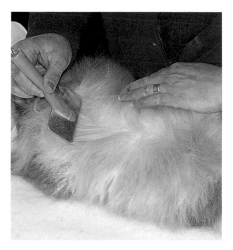

5 Carefully comb or cut out with scissors any knots that remain. The coat should be very soft, silky and free of tangles.

6 Now turn the cat over and then brush the long fur underneath, teasing out any knots with your fingers or a comb.

Claw trimming

As well as regularly grooming your cat's coat, you should examine his claws once every month. It may be necessary to trim them once or twice a year if they are over-long and he does not wear them down naturally outdoors or on indoor scratching sites.

Trimming a cat's claws should only be undertaken by a confident owner with appropriate claw cutters. Never be too severe when trimming them – only the tips should be trimmed. Never cut to the 'quick'. The pinkish area of each claw or quick is linked to a nerve ending and blood supply and should never be cut. If the claws are over-grown, consult your vet to prevent the risk of pain and suffering from over-cutting. An indoor cat should always be provided with several scratching post sites to prevent, or re-direct, scratching on pieces of furniture.

Eyes and ears

A cat's eyes should always be bright and healthy. Any clouding, excessive moisture or revealing of the third eyelid may suggest infection or damage, and your cat should be referred immediately to your vet. It should not be necessary to clean your cat's eyes unless an infection has developed and your vet has prescribed a specific treatment.

It is useful to wipe the inside of your cat's ears on a weekly basis to prevent a build-up of dirt that could provide a home for ear mites (see page 146). Only the immediate inner area of the ear should be wiped; do this in an outwards motion with a moist cotton wool ball. Do not ever insert sticks of cotton wool into the ear as this can cause serious damage to the inner ear.

Always clean away from a cat's eye, never over it, or you could damage the third eyelid.

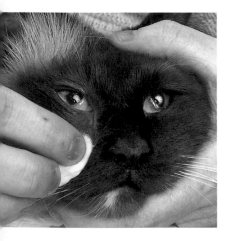

There should never be any discharge from the ears. If this happens, consult your vet. Look out for signs of a mite infection; the tell-tale symptoms are when a cat is continually scratching its head.

Oral hygiene

Cats in the wild keep their gums and teeth clean by eating prey, which needs to be chewed and crunched. However, in a domestic environment, many cats are only given processed, moist food. This 'soft option' diet offered over a cat's lifetime can lead to gum and teeth infections. Eventually teeth can be lost, and secondary infections in the bloodstream can even lead to major organ failure and an early demise.

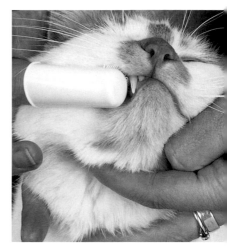

Even cats need their teeth cleaned to prevent tooth decay. You can buy special 'brushes' to make this process easier.

Preventing tooth decay

It is possible to prevent tooth decay in your cat by introducing an element of non-soft food into his diet. Some dried foods are promoted as being good for a cat's teeth because they have to be crunched and mimic the feline's natural diet in the wild. This action will help to keep the gums and teeth clean.

Some special cat toothpastes and toothbrushes are available from your vet or pet store. These can be used on a daily basis to reduce bacterial build-up, and tartar and plaque forming. Regular brushing will help prevent tooth decay and gum disease just as it does in humans. A weekly brush will ensure that your cat's teeth sparkle and that his breath does not prevent you from 'talking' directly to him.

Dire-smelling breath in your cat is usually a result of mouth infections, in particular gingivitis which can result in bleeding of the gums.

Feeding and drinking

Cats are notoriously fussy about their food, and they can be obsessively attentive about the cleanliness of dishes. All food, especially frozen or refrigerated, should be prepared in advance and offered to your pet at room temperature. Warming food replicates the temperature of prey in the wild.

must know

Water store
Some owners find it best to store tap water in a plastic container in order to bring it to room temperature and to reduce chlorine levels. Water is accepted better by cats if it has been allowed to stand for a day or so before use. Storage will allow the chlorine in tap water to dissipate with the oxygen that leaves the water as it warms to room temperature. Do not be surprised if your cat actively seeks out other sources of water. Cats are often attracted to running tap water, toilet water, ponds or puddles of dirty water.

General guidelines

Your cat's food dishes should be cleaned thoroughly on a daily basis, and fresh water must be added to the water bowl once or twice per day, depending on the number of visits your cat makes for water. Cats who are fed mainly dried foods will usually require more water than those who are offered canned or semi-moist foods. This is because the latter food types contain a high percentage of moisture and/ or water, and thus a cat who is fed them would not need to drink as frequently.

Feeding times

A cat who is older than six months can have food offered morning, afternoon and evening. To reduce any fussiness towards food, it is best to put the food dish down in the usual place and to ring a bell to signal that it's feeding time. Lift the dish up after 15 minutes; if the food has not been touched, cover it with cling film to preserve freshness and offer it again later. A healthy cat will soon begin to respond subconsciously to a sound signal for food. Some hungry cats will be at your feet as soon as the food can or packet is opened. The combination of smell and the behavioural cue of a rustling bag or packet can be enough of a signal for many cats to arrive in your kitchen. A cat's impatience will often result in him calling enthusiastically for you to serve up the evening meal.

Diet

Cats are true carnivores and, as avid meat eaters, they will rarely relish a diet that is not based on their needs. Indeed, kittens will not experience their ideal growth if they are fed on a diet that is based on vegetarian ingredients.

Cats instinctively search out variations in their diet. All their hunting and balancing skills have been evolved for them to be successful in their search for a meaty dinner. In the wild, this meat diet would range from small birds and mammals to a wide range of insects and invertebrates and scavenged carcasses. By eating such prey, cats obtain many variations of food, including blood, bones, feathers, fur and even crunchy exoskeletons.

By contrast, in domestication, a cat's diet can be rigid and repetitive, although good manufacturers attempt to replicate a cat's natural diet in their choice of ingredients. Although eating and feeding times do become habitualized in most domesticated pets, cats do not lose their natural instinct to seek out variations in their diet. This aspect of behaviour is displayed in an apparent fussiness or a dislike of food that was taken greedily and once seen to be satisfying.

Cats will often drink what looks like dirty water but they will only drink it if the top layer is clean.

Healthy cats need a balanced diet to keep them in good condition.

Outdoor cats enjoy hunting and prowling outside at night. Most cats hunt at dawn and at dusk.

Only the best

Cats will home in on any fresh food. They would eat only the best-quality steak and fish if that was on offer. With such a protein-rich diet, however, they would be missing essential vitamins and minerals and roughage. Having the equivalent of chocolate at every meal may sound appealing at first but this food will not offer a healthy, balanced diet.

It is important to rotate food types to offer a wide range to your cat and to help prevent any potential fussiness over food. Sometimes the variation can be created with complete dried foods, canned food, semi-moist food and tasty titbits of fresh fish, prawns and shreds of meat. These treats should be partially cooked or blanched to offer your cat the opportunity to chew his food.

Feeding guide for semi-adult to adult cats

Age	Type of cat	'Solid food' requirements
9–12 months	Kitten	Feed 2–3 times daily (first titbit, one dry, the other moist)
12–36 months	Active cat	Feed 2–3 times daily (first titbit, one dry, the other moist)
	Indoor cat	Twice daily (one dry, one semi-moist/titbit)
3–5 years	Active cat	Twice daily (one dry, one semi-moist or treats – strips of natural titbits, fish/fatty minced meat)
	Indoor cat	Once daily (complete dry food with small amounts of natural titbit treats)
5 years+	Active cat	Twice daily (one complete dry or semi-moist – small amounts, twice daily; one complete dry or semi-moist plus small natural titbits, and one titbit meal)
	Indoor cat	Once daily (complete dry 'mature cat' food) plus occasional treats

Note: The amount of food and the frequency of meals will depend, to some extent, on whether you own an indoor or outdoor cat. An active outdoor cat's nutritional requirements are greater than those of an inactive cat. Judge the quantity needed on the basis of consumption. If an amount is taken readily and immediately, gradually increase the quantity until the cat leaves some in the dish. This is better than offering a large meal only to find that much of it is left.

Feeding patterns should be scheduled evenly over the day. Night-time sleeping patterns can be encouraged by making the last meal more substantial than the others. Cats are naturally 'crepuscular' (active at dawn and at dusk), although some 'hunter personalities' will prefer to be active in darkness.

Using a litter tray

After all the eating and variation in your cat's diet, there will be 'smelly' by-products in the form of urine and faeces. Whether you have an indoor or an outdoor cat, he will need a litter tray.

must know

Positioning the tray
Where the litter tray is situated is important if the cat is going to be encouraged to use it in preference to other sites in the house. Choose a quiet place away from busy traffic areas as cats like to be private when they go to the toilet. Do not place it near feeding and water bowls or the dog's basket for obvious hygiene reasons.

Outdoor cats

Certainly, for indoor cats, a litter tray is essential, and although the outdoor cat will often urinate and defecate in the great beyond, there may be some instances, such as when he gets accidentally trapped in the house or at night-time, when his outdoor pursuits are restricted. On these occasions, a litter tray is more preferable as a site to deposit waste than your dining room carpet, so it's a good idea to provide one for an outdoor cat.

Cleaning the litter tray

It is essential to keep a cat's litter tray clean. Cats are meticulously clean creatures and prefer their toilet to be spotless! There are many different kinds of litter for you to choose from and they all vary slightly in texture, composition and weight.

Clumping litter is lightweight and economical to use as only the soiled litter needs to be removed and replaced. Once a day, using a scoop, you can sift through the litter and then remove any soiled material. You can replace the litter that has been removed with some more fresh litter.

However, it is still advisable occasionally to remove all the contents, wash the tray and then refill it. Always wash your hands thoroughly after this cleaning process to promote good hygiene.

Play

It's good for you to interact with your cat through play. Whatever toys you offer, he will find his own playthings. Play has its roots in hunting, stalking and pouncing, and many cats will play quite happily with an empty box, a carrier bag or even dead spiders!

Suitable toys

Set aside a few moments for play at least once a day. You can make your own 'toys' – some feathers tied together and drawn or dangled on a string will lure a healthy cat into play. The variation of 'prey on a string' can even include an enticing fresh food treat.

Games can be played without you. These include toy mice, ping pong balls, wool and catnip soft toys. Cats may play in short bursts or intense sessions. A visit to your local pet store will quickly show you the vast range of toys that are available. Track toys, where the cat sends a ball around a circular track, are popular, as are feather toys, 'fishing rod' types and roll-along toys.

must know

Sleepy cats
Cats can spend 60 per cent of a day sleeping. They will seek out warm and comfortable places, which may not include the lovely bed you have purchased for your pet. Because cats often seek height for security and warmth for comfort, they may 'disappear' to sleep in your airing cupboard or laundry basket, on shelves above radiators and on the top of cupboards. Don't be alarmed as it is perfectly normal for cats.

Encouraging play with your cat can create a positive interaction. Make time for play every day.

Identification

It is vital that your cat has some means of identification on his collar or through a recognized, widely used electronic method. You may lose your pet and, without some identification, the finder would be unable to locate and reunite you with your cat.

must know

Indoor cats
Even if you own a house cat who never ventures outside on his own, he will need some form of identification. Indoor cats can sometimes escape through open doors or windows, so fit yours with a collar or get him microchipped.

Microchipping

If your cat is to have access to the outside world, beyond your home and garden, then it is vital to provide him with some means by which he can be identified and returned to your home address. One of the most effective methods that is available today is microchipping. This process involves implanting a microchip, with the aid of a special hand-held unit, into the neck of your cat. The tiny microchip has your own unique identification code programmed into it. This registration number is then added to a computer data base which can be accessed by veterinarians, relevant animal rescue groups and authorities.

A secure method
In an emergency, should your cat become lost or injured, a hand-held scanner can be used to identify your code. Armed with this information, which can be accessed through the Pet Log data base, an enquirer would be able to obtain your name, address and contact telephone number, so that your cat could be returned safely to you. Unlike cat collars, which can become detached from your pet, the microchip implant is always secure, and it will provide a permanent identification method.

Cat collars

Collars are the most economical way of attaching an identification disc, tag or fob to your cat. The best ones are made from leather or a man-made durable material and should be fitted lightly rather than tightly onto the neck. A contact number or abbreviated address can be engraved onto a disc or placed inside a barrel holder. Many collar types are available, although quick release or safety variations with an elasticated section are the safest products. Either type is certainly worth the investment.

A young kitten, who is restricted to the home, could be given a soft material collar (not a flea collar) until used to wearing one. Once established as everyday wear, collars can be upgraded in size as the cat grows into an adult. Soft flea collars are designed for semi-adult to adult cats and are not suitable for kittens. There is a danger of a soft collar becoming hooked on a pointed object which could create a restriction and even lead to strangulation.

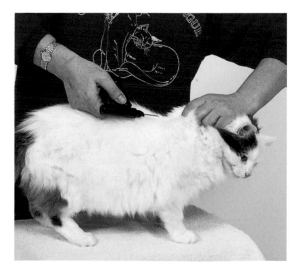

Microchipping your cat will ensure his identity can be quickly established in an emergency.

Car travel

To make sure that your cat becomes used to car journeys and travelling in a carry box, take him on short trips, perhaps to the supermarket or a local town, from three months onwards.

Desensitization

One of the first journeys your cat will make will be to your veterinary clinic for his vaccinations. Prior to these two separate immunization vaccinations, your kitten would not normally be allowed outside. It is always wise to desensitize your cat by allowing him to enter and exit the carry box freely over a period of a few weeks. Put an old item of your clothing inside. This could be 'scented' by adding it to your laundry basket of clothes to be washed. Your cat will associate with your scents and feel secure.

Practice makes purrfect

It is advisable never to make your cat's first car journey the one to the veterinary clinic, as this may give him a nasty association with car travel – his only other car experience probably being when you removed him from his mother and littermates. If a cat only travels in the car to receive a jab from a hypodermic needle, then it is not surprising if he makes the wrong association with car trips and you encounter problems in the future.

Do not feed your cat before going on a car journey as there is always a chance that he will regurgitate food if he becomes distressed. Larger carry boxes or travel crates will usually take a drip-feed water bottle; otherwise, make sure there is a dish of water in case he becomes thirsty. Ideally, place your cat in his carry box and transfer this to the back seat or hatchback space. Use a secure harness or a seat belt. Otherwise, place some solid item against the carry box to prevent any sudden shift should you have to brake sharply to stop the car.

Short but sweet

Keep the first few journeys relatively short, and on your return home, allow your cat to exit the carry box at his own pace. Make sure that he has some special treats in a saucer and access to water outside the box. This can make the experience of travelling in a car and being placed in a carrier less of a trauma for the cat. These short trips should be undertaken three or four times per week.

If your cat shows little sign of distress, then build up the journeys gradually into significant trips that you make on a regular basis. Always make sure that your car is well ventilated and also that there is no chance of temperature extremes. On hot summer days, your cat could quickly succumb to heat exhaustion in a car. In the winter, extreme cold could cause hyperthermia.

Preparing your cat for car journeys in this way will pave the way for successful future trips should you ever wish to use a cattery, move home or need to go to the veterinary clinic.

A carry box will be essential for transporting your cat safely. Make it cosy and allow your cat to explore it outside of visits to the vet to prevent a 'negative' association being formed.

Moving house

House moves can be traumatic enough for humans who know the reasons for relocating, whether for work or to upgrade for a growing family. However, cats have no idea why a move from one house to another is necessary and, as they are territorial by nature, the process of moving can be doubly traumatic.

must know

Orientating a cat
Spend several weeks 'orientating' your cat to your new home and neighbourhood rather than rush the process in the first week and risk losing him. Some cats who will walk on a harness can be guided around the block, if they have been accustomed to lead-walking from an early age.

Keep it simple

You can make a house move for your cat as smooth as possible by taking a few simple precautions. Do not wait until the last moment to place your cat in a carrier or travel crate. If you are chasing him around the home when the house keys are about to be handed in, then everyone will be stressed.

Indoor cats

The process of relocating is made much easier if you have a house-bound cat. Confine the cat in one room for about 24 hours prior to the day of moving. Keep any food given down to a bare minimum and leave the carrying box or travel crate available for the cat to enter and exit freely. It is best to end up with a hungry cat who is ready to eat once the move has been made because this will help prevent any potential travel sickness and make eating in the new home a priority – there is nothing like a hearty meal to make a cat feel at home.

Place one of your old sweaters, which has either been worn for a day or has been kept in the 'to be washed' laundry basket, inside the carrier or crate on moving day. Your cat can curl up on it and will be reassured by the familiar scent.

Outdoor cats

If your cat is a wanderer, do not risk trying to locate him on moving day. The absence of your cat at the moment of the actual relocation could lead to abandoning him accidentally, and also needless worry. Just keep the wanderer inside for about 24 hours prior to the move. Close the cat flap if you have one and confine him to one room together with all his needs – his litter tray, food, water and bedding. Harden your heart and ignore any cries to be released. Restricting him to one room will help condition him to living in a confined space in your new home. This is necessary while he has to adjust to a new home as well as new territory. When you are ready to move (all the furniture is in the van), enter the room and close the door behind you. Place your cat in the carrier or travel crate and then gather up your accessories to take with you.

Small is beautiful

When you arrive at your new home, whether your pet is an indoor or outdoor cat, select a small room where he can be placed, together with his used litter tray, food and water dishes. Cats will feel more 'secure' in a reduced territory as there is less to defend. They will seek a bolt hole when the world around them is perceived as threatening or unfamiliar.

Wait for a short time before opening the carrier door. Allow the cat to exit when he is ready and let him explore the room without any fuss. Pop in occasionally to offer a stroke or a special food treat, but beware of him making a dash for the nearest exit – many cats get lost in house moves.

Start with the carry box and let your cat explore his new home, taking each room one at a time.

Cats are territorial by nature and they find house moves disturbing. Follow the guidelines to ensure that your cat is secure before and after removal to your new home.

Over a few days, gradually open up the house to your cat, allowing him to explore. Prevent initial access to the garden or street because he may become disorientated in unfamiliar territory. There will be unknown roads, potentially aggressive rivals for the territory and many other dangers. The next week or two should consist of a gradual exploration of home, garden and neighbourhood, all under your guidance. Tinkle a bell with a name call to announce meals or treat times on a random basis and then you can call your cat at any time, using this signal.

Never trust an outdoor cat to make a 'mental map' of your new home and surroundings. This is a gradual process and the new territory needs to be 'written' over the old territory if he is not to become lost in the first days of exploration. Some cats will try to return to their familiar territory and they can become disorientated.

Going to the cattery

There are several reasons why cats may need to be housed in a boarding cattery, including family holidays, when a house move is not straightforward or when there is no one to take care of the cat in the event of the owner's hospitalization. He may need to board for just a few days or even several weeks.

Going away

The best option for your cat is to remain at home if possible with a relative, friend or a neighbour feeding him every day. If this is not an option, then using boarding catteries may be the only solution. Your vet may be able to recommend a suitable cattery or you can look through the local directories to find one nearby. Always be sure to inspect the establishment before leaving your cat. Although some boarding kennels also board cats, it is wise to look for a specialized cattery unless your cat is familiar with dogs and barking.

Holiday jabs

Make sure that your cat has been immunized or given booster jabs to prevent any health problems. A travel crate or carry box is essential for boarding because it offers your cat a part of his territory when he stays at the cattery. Never hold your cat whilst travelling or during the transfer from car to cattery because of the potential for panic and escape. The cattery is unlikely to be near your home and, as such, represents a new territory that is unknown to your cat. Don't fuss over him before he goes or on his return because this can highlight the separation.

want to know more?

• For advice on feeding cats, owners' common questions and answers, log on to the Feline Advisory Bureau website: www.fabcats.org
• To view Collins' other books on looking after adult cats, visit: www.collins.co.uk

weblinks

• You can buy cat safety collars online at: www.petplanet.co.uk
• All aspects of owning a cat are covered on: www.bluecross.org.uk

4 Good cat behaviour

One of the main factors in establishing and also maintaining a successful relationship is being able to communicate, but when the two participants in a relationship speak two completely different languages this may prove to be somewhat problematic. This is certainly the case in the relationship between man and cat, and one very important step in improving relationships between cats and their owners is teaching the owners to understand the subtle signals that make up feline communication.

Communication systems

Cats use three major systems of communication in order to get their message across. By studying these systems and by learning to interpret feline signals accurately, owners can begin to view the world from a more feline perspective.

The three systems

Vocalization, visual signalling and olfactory (scent) communication all combine to make the cat a very effective communicator, and the development of each of these systems can be better understood when feline communication is considered within the context of its behavioural needs.

Avoiding confrontation

For many years the cat was regarded as an asocial animal, but recently this solitary image has been questioned. Research has shown that cats do engage in affiliative social interactions with other members of their own species and also that they can form worthwhile social relationships with the humans in their world.

However, independence is still an important feature of feline life and, when it comes to hunting, cats do work very much on their own. One of the consequences of being a solitary hunter is that cats are highly motivated to avoid physical conflict and potential injury and keep themselves fit enough to seek out prey. As a result, they have developed a varied and fascinating language, which is designed specifically to diffuse tension and, in feline terms, confrontation is most definitely a last resort.

Opposite: Cats' eyes are very expressive and the size of their pupils can denote contentment, excitement or even fear.

Scent marking

Scent (olfactory) signals are specific to the individual cat. They are stable over a period of time and can be deposited in the cat's environment and detected and decoded by another cat at a later date, in the absence of the individual who deposited them.

must know

Scent signals
It is almost impossible for us to appreciate the value of olfaction in social interactions since we rely on visual and vocal communication, and our sense of smell is so limited that we cannot appreciate the subtleties of the odours around us. Depositing scent signals is called marking, and there are four basic forms of this behaviour in the domestic cat: rubbing, scratching, urine marking and middening (see page 95).

Accuracy is essential

Marking has distinct advantages for the cat, and scent signalling plays an important role in avoiding confrontation and maintaining distance. However, the major disadvantage of odour communication is that alteration of the signal is difficult to achieve and once the message has been left it cannot be rapidly removed, should that become necessary. This means that cats need to be accurate in their olfactory signalling, and it is believed that most of the information contained in scent deposits is of a factual rather than an emotional nature.

The cat is highly adapted to deposit scent signals, and special scent-producing glands are located on its body. The major areas of scent production are the face, flanks and tail base, but cats also have glands on the paws, which deposit scent signals during the process of scratching, and they will utilize the scent of urine and faeces as a form of communication.

The scent signals a cat deposits help to identify it to other cats, both within its social group and in the wider community, and give important information about how long ago the individual was in the area. Time-scheduling is a very important feature of feline life, especially in areas of high population density, such as housing estates.

Cats that are forced to share relatively small territories use scent signals to communicate with fellow felines and inform them of how long ago they used any specific passage track within the territory, avoiding the need for any face-to-face encounters.

Reading scent signals

To interpret scent signals, cats rely not only on their sense of smell but also on a chemical sense – a combination of taste and smell. This is mediated by the Jacobson's organ, which is situated in the hard palate and accessed via two small openings in the mouth behind the upper incisor teeth. These ducts lead to two fluid-filled, blind-ending sacs lined with olfactory cells. Scent is forced up into the ducts by pressing the tongue against the roof of the mouth.

In order to achieve this, the cat engages in a specific behaviour, which is known, as the flehmen reaction. Cats performing a flehmen response have a characteristic appearance, and they will stretch their neck, open their mouth, wrinkle their nose and curl back their lip in what almost resembles a snarl.

When cats encounter new scent signals they will spend some time sniffing at the marks and interpreting the message.

Rubbing

Owners will frequently see their cat using the specialized scent glands of their face and flanks to deposit signals on inanimate objects in the house and garden, on other cats in the household and even on their owners themselves. What does this mean?

must know

Rubbing on legs
When domestic cats rub up against their owners' legs, they are not only acknowledging status and confirming the stability of the owner/ cat relationship, but they are also picking up and depositing scent in order to establish a common signal, which can then be used to identify members of the same social group and reassure individuals that they belong.

Stable relationships

Many owners encourage their pets to rub around their legs. This full-body rubbing is a form of greeting behaviour, usually accompanied by an erect tail, which signals a desire to interact. Rubbing is one of the important affiliative behaviours which work to maintain stability within a feline community. Within the pet-owner relationship, this behaviour is often reinforced as a greeting ritual by the owner's response. Rubbing behaviour between cats is usually initiated by the weaker individual, and although cats do not live in a structured hierarchy, rubbing does appear to be important in acknowledging status as well as exchanging scent.

Cats use the scent glands on their face to leave messages for other cats in the neighbourhood, and to reassure themselves that their territory is secure.

Scratching

The sight of a cat stropping its front claws on a fence panel in the garden is a familiar one to most people, but the simplicity of this behaviour masks its complexity in terms of feline communication. Misinterpreting this can lead to tension between cat and owner.

Healthy claws

Most cat owners interpret scratching as being a purely functional behaviour and they believe that the cat is sharpening his claws. Certainly scratching is an important form of manicure for cats, and it is essential to keep their claws in trim in order for them to hunt successfully.

Removing claw sheaths

However, rather than sharpening the existing claw, the cat is actually removing the blunted outer claw sheath in order to reveal a glistening new weapon underneath, and the discarded outer claw coverings are often to be found at the bottom of a cat's favourite scratching locations.

Strong muscles

Another extremely important functional role of scratching is to exercise and to strengthen the cat's muscles as well as the tendons that play an important part in protracting the claws. It is very important for your cat to practise this regularly in order to keep his claws ready for action, not only during the kill but also when he is climbing trees and fence panels or perhaps defending himself in a confrontation with another cat.

must know

Marking
The third function of scratching is marking. Scratch posts can act as a visual marker, and the vertical scratch marks communicate with other neighbourhood cats. They also act as scent signposts. Under a cat's paws are small scent glands, and the rhythmic stropping of the feet along the post activates these glands to deposit their signal. The sweat glands release their secretion, resulting in a unique scent mark.

Urine marking

Spraying urine as a signal of communication is a deliberate behaviour, and it is very important to distinguish this from the evacuation of urine from a full bladder during urination.

A set routine

Cats can deposit urine marks regardless of the state of their bladder, and they perform this behaviour in a set routine, during which the area they spray and the number of squirts remain constant, despite fluctuations in the amount of liquid they deposit.

One of the reasons why cats perform urine spraying from a standing position is to deposit the urine at nose height where it will be readily noticed by other cats. However, they may also mark with urine which they deposit from a squatting position.

Despite a popular belief that this behaviour is limited to tom cats, it is now recognized that most cats deposit urine around the periphery of their

When cats urinate in the open and don't attempt to cover their deposits, it is likely that they are using the urine to communicate.

outdoor territory on a regular basis and that cats of either sex will use this urine marking as an important communication tool, regardless of whether they have been neutered.

Functions of urine marking

One of the primary purposes of urine marking in the outdoor territory is to operate a time-share system, ensuring that the available territory is not over-hunted and minimizing contact between unfamiliar cats. When it is performed by sexually active male and female cats, it is used to signal the female's receptivity and to draw the cats closer together.

Tom cats pay great attention to the marks of in-oestrus females as they contain information about the stage of oestrus and the likelihood of mating. One important feature of sexually-related spraying is that cats engaging in this behaviour will often vocalize as they deposit their signal. Obviously, this form of marking is only encountered in entire cats, and it can be readily controlled by neutering.

It was thought that spraying was the mark of an over-confident cat using the scent as a threatening signal to others. However, the reactions of other cats to the spray marks do not appear to be fear-related and cats are often drawn to the marks and sniff at them with great interest. Many cats sniff at the sprayed area and simply walk away, apparently unaffected by the message, while others spray over the mark with their own urine, responding to the information by confirming they are also in the area. Insecure individuals will also use the behaviour to reassure themselves; by spreading around their own distinctive odour these cats become more confident.

Body language

Cat watching is a fascinating occupation but in order to get the most out of the cat-owner relationship it is helpful to know a little more about the messages that your cat is giving when he changes his body position and facial expression.

must know

Developing skills
Understanding your cat takes practice, and interpreting his body language is made even more challenging by the high degree of individuality involved. However, developing the skill of recognizing and translating basic feline expressions will help enormously in cat-human communication.

Interpreting the signals

Accurate interpretation of your cat's body language not only makes the relationship more rewarding, but it also reduces the potential for misunderstandings, enabling you to predict your cat's behaviour and avoid unnecessary conflict. The cat's overall posture gives the first indication as to his intentions and how confident or insecure he is feeling. Readiness to run is a good indicator of intentions, since flight is his primary defence strategy, and when there is a hint of danger or confrontation his instinct is to flee.

Cats try to avoid conflict, and a certain amount of bluffing is allowed if it increases a cat's chances of survival. However, this can only be done safely

Body language is an important method of communication in feline encounters. The cat on the right is preparing to escape whilst maintaining its ability to defend itself if necessary.

from a distance where the truth is unlikely to be discovered. Arching the back, raising the hair on the back and over the tail, and standing at an angle to the perceived threat are acceptable ways for cats to lie about their size and make their opponent think twice about taking them on. In many cases, this bluff can be successful and cats retreat before they get close enough to discover the truth. Sometimes, however, the potential threat continues to advance and the cat needs to reconsider its position. If a change of plan is required, the sideways posture enables it to keep its opponent in view whilst retreating slowly to avoid inducing a chase response.

Honesty is the best policy

For some cats, honesty is still the best policy, and when they feel threatened they take avoiding action and retreat. If the opportunity arises, this retreat will involve physically leaving the conflict situation and getting far away, but if this is not an option the cat will shrink to its smallest possible size and try to hide. In some cases, the cat may get under or behind a physical barrier. However, cats truly believe that if they can't see you, you can't see them and simply avoid eye contact and turn their back on the threat.

Facial signals

Although the overall body posture of a cat can be very important in assessing his intentions in any form of interaction, it is the facial expressions that give a more accurate impression of his emotional state and provide the fine tuning in feline visual communication. Anyone who has worked with cats in situations where they are potentially stressed and

The averted eyes and crouched posture suggest that this cat is trying to avoid interaction.

Although ear positions can be important indicators of a cat's emotional state, it is important to consider them in the context of other signals to ensure that they are interpreted accurately.

under pressure will know how important it is to keep an eye on a cat's face to determine what he is likely to do next. Some feline expressions of fear and anger can be similar and before interpreting the signals from individual components, e.g. the eyes, ears or tail, it is essential to put each of them into the context of a cat's total body language.

What do the ears tell you?

Cats can change their ear positions with remarkable speed. This is not only useful from a predatory point of view to aid the detection of moving prey but also important in communication. Cats use small ear movements to assess the potential reaction of any opponent, and during any single encounter the ear position of each cat may alter several times.

A cat with ears facing forwards is confident and alert, and even when the ears are tilted slightly back most individuals are still happy and relaxed. But if the ears are flattened, interpreting the ear position is not so easy. As the potential for confrontation increases, the ears are gradually moved back and flattened against the head, but avoid jumping to conclusions at this stage. Flattening the ears is an important precaution in any form of confrontation, regardless of whether the individual is the aggressor or the victim, since the ears are vital instruments of communication and need to be protected from potential damage in the ensuing fight. Ears that are folded sideways and downwards indicate the cat is trying to avoid confrontation and preparing to defend itself from an approaching threat. A cat whose ears are flattened against the head with a backwards rotation is getting ready to attack.

What big eyes you have!

Feline eyes are very expressive and the size of the pupils is a good indicator as to emotional state. It is important to take into account all of the available information when trying to interpret eye signals. Dilated pupils are commonly associated with fear, whereas narrowed apertures may be a sign of contentment. However, large pupils can also result from non-fearful arousal, such as excitement, and observing the cat's overall behaviour is important. The level of lighting should also be considered when observing pupil size; the behavioural significance of large pupils in situations of low-light intensity or narrow pupils in bright light needs to be questioned.

What are you looking at?

When cats deliberately seek or avoid eye contact there is a message in their behaviour. Slow blinking is usually the sign of a relaxed and happy cat, but when blinking is used in communication between cats and their owners and between cats themselves it is a way of seeking reassurance and avoiding confrontation. Staring, on the other hand, is the sign of a very assertive individual, and prolonged eye contact can be used to intimidate an opponent.

It has often been reported that cats will seek out people who do not like them, and when owners have company they often find their pet making a beeline for the one person in the room who finds cats unappealing. People who do not like cats will usually avoid direct eye contact and narrow their eyes, whereas those who want to initiate interaction with the cat will actively make eye contact with them. In feline terms, the cat lover appears to be

A cat's eyes can provide you with valuable information about his state of mind and behaviour.

staring in a confrontational manner and is likely to be avoided whereas the person trying to avoid any eye contact is giving clear signals that they are not a threat and can therefore be trusted!

Tail signals

The role of the cat's tail in feline communication has often been overlooked. However, it is now recognized that it is an important factor in social communication as well as an expression of the cat's emotional state.

Speed of movement

This can give us some important clues as to a cat's intention in any interaction. A rapid, thrashing tail movement is generally associated with arousal, while graceful, slow sweeping is seen as a sign of contentment. There is an established belief that a wagging tail is a sign of extreme annoyance and anger but this is not necessarily the case, and rapid movement of the tail simply indicates that the cat is agitated and in a state of emotional conflict. If people ignore this signal and continue to advance towards the cat, this may well result in confrontation but it does not necessarily prove that the cat is either bad tempered or aggressive.

Flight is always the preferred defence strategy of the cat, and this individual is ready to spring out of the way if the perceived threat gets too close.

Saying hello

The tail is very expressive since not only is it capable of a whole range of movements – up and down and from side to side – but also the tip can be moved independently of the base. During greeting, cats use their tail position to test out the potential reaction of the other individual and avoid rejection.

An upright tail is a friendly gesture that signals a non-threatening approach. If used as a prelude to rubbing it is a request for permission to interact and an important way of ensuring that the interaction that follows is friendly. A raised tail also signals an intention to discover more about the other cat as it exposes the genital region and invites the other individual to sniff underneath and find out all about that cat. As well as holding the tail high, cats will also alter the position of the tail tip during greeting, and the way in which the tip is bent over appears to be very specific to the individual.

Displaying emotion

Tail position is not only important during social greeting, and a lot can be learnt by observing the tail during other feline activities, including sexual encounters and aggressive displays. Queens will move their tail to allow toms to receive the full impact of their scent communication and inform them that they are ready for mating, whereas aggressive cats may use concave and lowered tail positions in order to indicate their intentions during a conflict. Sometimes the signals from the tail can be very subtle and quite difficult to interpret, but one exception is the fluffed-up bottle brush tail, which is a signal associated with fear and defence.

When a cat approaches with an erect tail and a bent tail tip, it is indicating its intention to engage in friendly interaction.

Social behaviour

In order to understand more about how cats interact with their owners, it is not only necessary to know about their methods of communication but also about their social behaviour and the ways in which they naturally interact with other cats.

must know

Group harmony
Maintaining harmony within any social group can be a challenge and family unity cannot be taken for granted in feline society. Cats have behavioural patterns that are designed to minimize the potential for conflict, including rubbing and grooming. As well as signalling affection, rubbing is a demonstration of feline respect.

Feline society

Cats live in a female-dominated society, and their social behaviour in the wild is based on co-operation between mothers, daughters, grandmothers, sisters and aunts who all live together in family units. Within these groups, the cats share the rearing of each other's kittens, and they assist one another in defending their territory from any potential intruders. Behaviour between group members is based on affection and tolerance, but outsiders are not welcome and the hostility shown towards individuals who do not belong can be very intense.

This can have serious implications in multi-cat households where cats are often expected to live with unrelated individuals. It is mainly due to the effect of neutering that such unnatural feline groupings can live together in relative harmony.

Integrating newcomers
Littermates make the best housemates, and when owners are setting up a new feline household it is advisable to keep related individuals together. Integration of newcomers is possible, provided that adequate attention is paid to natural feline social behaviour and that the introductions are made only in a gradual and non-threatening manner.

Mutual grooming

Unlike rubbing, grooming is a more reciprocal social behaviour, which is used to cement relationships between cats and exchange social information in the form of tastes and smells. Allogrooming (mutual grooming) is not restricted to the head and neck, which are areas that a cat may find difficult to keep clean. As well as grooming one another, most cats will sniff the head and the tail region of their close companions, especially when they have been apart. It is believed that by doing so they check up on the activities of their housemates while they have been away. By detecting the scents with which the returning cat has come into contact, it is possible to discover what the individual has been eating as well as where he has been and who he has been with.

When cats develop mutually rewarding relationships, owners can gain a great deal of pleasure from watching them together.

Natural behaviour

Although the cat is classed as a domesticated animal, it is widely believed that the process of domestication is still not complete, especially as cats retain so much of their wild behaviour.

must know

A good owner
The most important quality in a cat owner is understanding their cat. Learning to see life from a feline perspective can take time, and it is important to recognize that the fundamental differences in our social behaviour and our communication systems can cause confusion. The feline senses are finely tuned to function in a world dominated by scent signals, many of which pass over the head of the owner.

How could he do that?

For many owners the prospect of their cat killing wildlife is distressing, and it is an ironic fact that many cat lovers are also interested in bird life and are very concerned about the issues of wildlife conservation. However, all cats need to hunt, and when they are kept within a domestic environment they are no less motivated to hunt and dispatch prey than when they are living in feral conditions.

The motivation to hunt has nothing to do with hunger. Attempts to limit the level of destruction by feeding cats more proprietary cat food are only successful when the cat becomes so overweight that he can no longer run fast enough to catch his prey! Even then the cat will still be tuned for the kill, and when movement and sound combine to trigger the natural instinct, he will go through the motions of the hunt even if he cannot catch his prey.

You can curtail your pet's hunting activities while still allowing him to be true to his heritage. All cats have an innate requirement to respond to the call of nature by hunting and dispatching prey of one sort or another, but there is plenty of opportunity for owners to control the source of that 'prey'. Cats can easily learn to hunt toys and owner-controlled food sources rather than wildlife. You just have to make the time to initiate this activity.

Playing is not simply for pleasure

Play is vital for cats, and every day they need to act out their natural behavioural sequences and practise the survival skills. Hunting lends itself to play, and by recognizing the way in which rapid movement and high-pitched sound trigger the natural hunting instinct, we can select toys that stimulate the same responses. It is important for cats to have the opportunity to catch and dispatch some of these prey items, and their toys must therefore be suitable for this purpose. In addition to triggering the hunt response, they must be able to withstand the outcome of that response and not run any risk of fragmenting or breaking when the cat attempts to kill them. In the wild, cats will spend up to six hours a day hunting, and therefore responsible owners need to be prepared to spend some time every day engaging in play with their pet.

Dawn and dusk are important for hunting, and many cats become more active at these times.

Training your cat

As in training other species, successful feline education relies on the correct application of reinforcement, and timing is a vital factor in teaching cats new tricks. The reward needs to arrive while the cat is actually performing the desired behaviour.

Successful training

Forcing cats to perform behaviours so that they can be rewarded is usually unsuccessful, and it is better to be prepared to wait for the desired response to occur spontaneously and then to reward it. However, this can lead to long time delays as well as a corresponding drop in owner enthusiasm. Another approach is to break the desired behaviour down into smaller components. This can be very successful since the individual tasks are slightly easier to perform than the ultimate goal and there is an increased probability that there will be an opportunity to reward. As each little step becomes established, the owner can then work to put them all together and eventually achieve their goal. Patience is the key to success.

Learning through reward

It is often assumed that training is simply not an option within the cat-owner relationship, and many owners resign themselves to all sorts of behaviours from their pets in the belief that there is simply nothing that they can do to teach them to behave in a more appropriate way. This is not the case, and cats can be trained to behave appropriately and to perform behaviours on command. However, the difficulty comes in identifying a reward that the cat will consider valuable enough to work for. Determining the best reward for an individual cat will involve watching its reactions and finding those things that appear to motivate it most. Some cats will work for games and for social interaction, but their independent social behaviour does not make human praise a very strong motivator.

In most cases, the successful feline rewards are food based. Very few cats will find their daily food ration rewarding, and in cat training it is more common to use treat-based foods, such as cheese, tuna and prawns. One important element of reward in cat terms is novelty, and whatever reward you select, it is very important to vary it from time to time in order to maintain your cat's interest in training and his motivation to comply.

Some cats, such as this regal Burmese, will quite happily wear a harness and they can be trained to walk successfully on a lead.

Using the cat flap

A good example of the application of incremental learning is teaching your cat to use a cat flap. This process will require time and patience, especially in the early stages. Few cats instinctively know how to react when they first encounter a cat flap, and they will need to learn that getting through the flap will bring them access to something worthwhile.

Once the behaviour has been established, the act of entering the house through the flap will be rewarded by the comfort of home, and the act of going out will be rewarded by access to outside, but in the early stages, an owner needs to provide much higher-value rewards, such as toys or food, in order to train a cat to use the flap successfully.

Keeping things positive

One of the most common approaches to cat flap training is to physically push the cat through the flap. However, for a creature that always likes to be in control, this method runs the risk of inducing negative associations with the flap and teaching the cat to avoid it rather than use it. A more successful approach is to prop the flap open so that the cat can see the great outdoors and be motivated to move through the flap with minimal resistance.

Rewarding the cat

In the early stages, it is best to teach the cat to come in rather than to go out, and the prospect of warmth and shelter can be used to encourage the cat to come inside. However, entry into the home is unlikely to be sufficiently rewarding, and the presence of a food reward or an exciting toy on the

must know

Priorities
These differ between our two species, and while we have a real need for a loving and nurturing relationship with our cats the feline perspective of the cat-human relationship is different. Cats can learn to enjoy our company and can make very rewarding companions, but they have no fundamental need for social interaction and this has significant implications in terms of owner expectation.

inside of the flap will usually be needed to persuade the cat that coming through the hole is really a sensible thing to do. Once movement through the open flap has been established, the next stage is for you to gradually lower the flap so that the cat needs to apply some pressure to open it.

This part of the procedure can be very slow and, as with all training, owners will need to be patient, remembering that losing their temper or becoming exasperated will only serve to make the process more distressing and even longer in the end.

Cat flaps are regarded by most owners as a very useful invention. However, cats will need to learn how to use them, and some will perceive them as a threat rather than as a luxury.

Curing behaviour problems

Behavioural therapy is just as relevant to the cat as it is to other species, such as dogs, and owners of problem cats now have access to an increasing amount of expertise in the field of feline behaviour. You can do a lot to prevent problem behaviours.

must know

The wrong context
Many cat behaviours that owners regard as a problem are actually perfectly normal when performed in the right context, such as hunting birds or spraying urine or scratching.

It's only natural

Many of the so-called problem behaviours that cats display are, in fact, perfectly normal, but they may create a problem for owners if they are performed within the home. Examples include urine spraying, scratching and hunting, all of which are part of the cat's natural behavioural repertoire.

Simply stopping cats from displaying these natural behaviours is not the answer, and it is important to look at the problem from a feline angle and try to understand why the behaviour is being performed in an abnormal context. Learning to understand the ways in which cats communicate and behave in the wild can often be the first step to dealing with and solving many of these common behaviour problems.

Ensuring that the cat's environment gives him the maximum opportunity to display his normal behaviours is often another important consideration when making behavioural treatment plans.

Anxiety and stress

While many common feline behaviour problems result from misunderstandings between our species, it is possible for cats to exhibit behavioural difficulties resulting from factors such as genetics, inappropriate rearing and the subsequent emotional trauma.

Opposite: Paying attention to your kitten's development can have a profound effect on the incidence of behavioural problems in adulthood.

Curing behaviour problems | 111

Cats and dogs are traditionally regarded as enemies, but by introducing them at an early age the two species can develop a close and lasting relationship.

Problems in each of these areas can leave some cats with an inability to deal with any novelty and challenges in the world around them, and this makes them prone to the negative effects of stress. In order to prevent these problems, it is important to appreciate the relevance of both genetic input and life experience to the behavioural development of the domestic cat and to work to ensure that all kittens are given the very best possible start in life ˋ in terms of both their socialization and habituation. Unfortunately, this is not always achieved, and anxiety and stress are common factors in the onset of feline behavioural disorders.

Take a trip to the vet

Not all cat behaviour problems are straightforward, and it is also important to remember that there is a very strong link between behaviour and physical health. A veterinary examination should always be performed when a cat behaves in an unacceptable or unexpected manner, and this is particularly important in those situations where cats begin to deposit either urine or faeces in the household.

Urinary tract disease can be a common factor in many cases of indoor toileting, and focusing on the behavioural issues before investigating the medical causes can lead to an unacceptable time delay and a potentially life-threatening deterioration in the health of the affected cat.

Investigating behaviour problems

Dealing with feline behaviour problems can be a time-consuming process, and it is important to determine the motivation for any inappropriate behaviour before attempting to draw up treatment plans for cats and their owners. This will require not only a large amount of empathy and patience but also a sound level of scientific knowledge. The theory behind the development, investigation and treatment of feline behaviour problems is outside the remit of this book. However, it is possible to give a brief overview of some of the common feline behaviour problems and provide some insight into how these problems can be treated. Any owners who have behavioural concerns about their pet should make an appointment to see their veterinary surgeon and seek one-to-one advice which can be tailored to their individual animal.

must know

Cats can learn, too
Problem behaviours can also develop through inappropriate learning, and this area is often overlooked in feline circles because of a mistaken belief that cats are untrainable. Not only are they capable of learning new associations through training but they are also very adept at training their owners. Unintentional provision of reward when a cat is behaving in an inappropriate manner can rapidly lead to a learned response that is difficult to remove.

Spraying and marking

Cats mark their territory in several ways, and whereas some of these marking behaviours are considered acceptable by owners, others are viewed as being antisocial in the extreme.

Antisocial behaviour?

Few owners will be offended by the sight of their cat rubbing his cheek against the stereo unit and many will encourage this form of scent exchange as part of the greeting ritual, but if the cat starts to leave his scent in the form of urine or faeces or scratches his message on the back of the brand new sofa it is a different story. From a feline perspective, there is little difference between any of these behaviours.

Identifying the trigger

When dealing with marking problems, treatment will depend on understanding why these messages are being misplaced. If the onset of the marking behaviour has been sudden, it may be relatively easy to pinpoint the trigger. However, in many cases the behaviour has been long-standing before owners attempt to remedy it, and in these situations the original trigger may be difficult to determine.

Identifying the locations for marking behaviour in chronological order often reveals a pattern, which helps in the identification of the original trigger even if that stimulus is no longer present. Once the cause has been identified, treatment is aimed at breaking the habit of indoor marking, controlling the cat's exposure to the challenge and working to increase his overall feeling of security.

Breaking the habit

Whatever the form of the marking behaviour, the cat will always be attracted to the signals he has deposited, and when he detects that the scent is decaying he will be compelled to top up his signal. This means that effective cleaning of marking locations is essential if the treatment is to be successful. Unfortunately, many household cleaners contain some ammonia and/or chlorine, and since these are constituents of cat urine, it is easy to see how confusion may arise in cases of indoor spraying.

The most efficient method for cleaning any sites of feline marking behaviour is to wash the area with a warm solution of a biological detergent and then, once the area is dry, scrub it down with surgical spirit or other alcohol. Check the fabric for colour fastness before using this regime – applying the treatment to a small test area before cleaning vast expanses of carpet is a sensible approach.

Deterrents

Once the area has been cleaned, it may be a good idea to place some deterrents in the places where marking has previously occurred. In general, the most effective deterrents are ones that are based on natural ways of redefining the function of the territory, increasing the cat's confidence and removing the need to mark.

The presence of food is a tried and tested method of identifying the home as a core territory which is safe and secure. Items of a cat's bedding or a variety of toys have been shown to have a similar effect. Likewise, the naturally occurring scent signals from the face of the cat can be beneficial in reassuring an

When cats scratch on trees, they are not only taking care of their claws but are also leaving clear visual and olfactory messages.

Feline scratching is a complex behaviour, but it can also develop as a learned response. For this cat, scratching at the carpet is rewarded if the door is opened.

individual of the security of its home. You can either use a facial cloth, which you rub across the face of your cat and then apply to previously marked areas within the house, or you can invest in a synthetic analogue of this scent signal, which is called Feliway, and apply this directly from the bottle. One very important thing to realize is that the cleaning regime already outlined (see page 115) can affect the activity of Feliway, and a period of 24 hours should elapse between cleaning and its application if you are to maximize your chances of success.

Obviously there is often a lot more to dealing with marking problems than cleaning and redefining the cat's territory, and if these simple measures do not prove effective then you will need to contact your veterinary surgeon for more advice.

Dealing with the cause

If treatment is going to offer hope of a long-term resolution of the problem, the approach to any form of marking problems must involve dealing with the cause of the behaviour. If it is possible to identify a specific stimulus which is acting as a trigger, then treatment should involve taking steps to isolate the cat from that challenge, at least in the short term.

Your long-term aim is to teach your cat to cope with challenges in his environment – physical or emotional – but you can isolate him from the source of his anxiety while another therapy is instituted to increase his confidence. For example, the entry of another cat into the home via a cat flap, whether actual or threatened, can be avoided by blocking the flap. Restricting your cat's access to areas of the home that are particularly challenging will also help.

What constitutes an unreasonable challenge is, of course, dependent on the individual cat, and things that the majority of cats may take in their stride may act as the trigger for a marking problem in a particularly sensitive individual.

Never punish your cat

Punishment should always be avoided. Often the cat is not actually caught in the act of marking, and retrospective punishment has no effect on the behaviour but merely serves to confuse the cat. Even when the owner does see the cat actually in the process of marking, punishment is not advised. The cat is behaving perfectly naturally in feline terms and, since stress and anxiety are often causes of these problems in the first place, punishment can only serve to increase the cat's stress level and may even make the behaviour worse.

Cat flaps can lead to a decrease in home security, especially if neighbouring cats use them too!

Fear and timidity

Although most cats tend to be confident and fearless hunters, some can develop behavioural problems associated with fear and anxiety, becoming over-dependent on their owners, fearful of strangers and anxious about venturing outside their homes.

When a new kitten is introduced, the resident cat will benefit from the provision of high-up resting places where he can retreat if the youngster is too overpowering.

Active and passive responders

Cats have two methods of dealing with situations in which they feel threatened.

• Active responders will make their feelings obvious and will respond to the presence of people they fear with vocalization and obvious distress. If an escape route is blocked, these cats are likely to resort to aggressive displays to repel the perceived threat, and the risk of injury from them is very real.

• Passive responders respond to their fear by withdrawing socially and emotionally from the world around them. They seek high resting places and shut themselves off from any interaction. They internalize their fear and are more at risk from developing behavioural problems, such as over-grooming, rather than showing overt aggression.

Inappropriate fear responses

Lack of appropriate socialization and habituation is the most common cause of these problems, but other factors, such as genetic input from the cat's father, observational and genetic input from the mother and learning as the result of insufficient, inappropriate or even hostile interaction with the surrounding environment and with people also need to be considered.

Unintentional learning

One of the effects of the efficient flight response in cats is that fearful escape behaviour is highly rewarding. If a cat feels threatened by someone and manages to run away, it learns that retreat is an effective means of limiting unwanted contact and will run sooner rather than later when the next encounter occurs. Cats are not highly motivated by rewards, such as food or play, and you need to work hard to encourage your cat to be the one to take the initiative. In this way the social interaction can become inherently rewarding, and food and play can be introduced as additional reinforcers.

Treatment

Preventing fear and timidity in cats, through adequate socialization and habituation and the appropriate selection of breeding stock, is obviously the ideal approach, but we also have to recognize that problems do arise and that a significant number of domestic cats are already suffering from inappropriate fear in reaction to their environment, to strangers or their owners. Whatever the actual manifestation of their fear, these cats need to be helped to overcome their problems by altering their perceptions and working to form positive associations with the world around them.

Punishment is never appropriate for them and over-reassurance should also be avoided. In some cases where the level of fear prevents the cat from learning new behaviours, short-term drug therapy may be needed, but such treatment should never be used in isolation and behavioural therapy methods will also be necessary. Ask your vet for advice.

must know

Back off

Owners need to back off and allow their cat to take control. Although you may want to help your cat overcome his fear, this approach may be counter-productive. It is better to work at making the world more attractive in feline terms and encourage the cat to seek interaction, since it is only once the cat actually wants to interact with his environment that he will be ready and able to overcome his fear.

Aggression towards cats

Cats are not confrontational animals by nature, and they have a very elaborate communication system, which is designed both to diffuse conflict and to avoid physical violence.

Fighting between cats living in the same household can be very distressing for their owners.

Territorial disputes

Between cats in the same household these are the exception rather than the rule, but problems are often encountered during the initial introduction. In a few rare cases, the cats never learn to co-habit peacefully, and the aggression between them can be extremely distressing for their owners.

Territorial disputes between neighbouring cats are relatively common, and sometimes a single cat can inflict a reign of terror over a neighbourhood. The consequences of this behaviour are not only measured in terms of injury to neighbouring cats but also the breakdown in friendly relations between human neighbours. Feline confrontation can easily escalate into full-scale neighbour disputes.

Neighbourhood problems

Despotic cats can be treated by increasing the perception of their home as a secure den so they spend more time there, and teaching them that other houses are out of bounds. Setting up a time-share system whereby the 'problem' cat has access to outdoor territory at times when the 'victims' are safely tucked up at home may seem like a cop-out but is an effective way of buying time and enabling the owners to get together to discuss what to do. Making the home of the 'victim' secure by fitting a coded cat flap is a simple step, but it is not always successful and some more experienced bullies are very adept at beating these devices and entering the home on the tail of a legitimate resident.

Making the 'victim's' home unwelcoming to the intruder is important, but it is sometimes difficult to do this in a way that does not make the house unappealing to the resident as well. Invading cats can quickly learn that the hostility is coming from the humans in the household, and when owner-driven deterrents, such as water pistols, are used, the despot will soon limit its break-ins to times when the owners are not about. Booby traps or deterrents that cannot be directly traced to the owners are therefore more effective, and, if the timing of their delivery is accurate, noise deterrents and water deterrents delivered with an element of surprise can have dramatic effects.

When a cat encounters a stranger in his own territory, then scent communication is very important in the introduction process.

Multi-cat households

In most cases, aggression between cats in the same household occurs when a newcomer arrives, but there are times when cats who have lived together for years suddenly fall out. The chances of conflict increase if one or more of the cats in the social group is poorly socialized or there is competition over resources. If there are many cats in a small house and a shortage of high-up resting places, if the owner has limited time to give them attention or if food supply is restricted, tension can rise and cats can become intolerant of their housemates. Other stressors within the environment can cause a breakdown in relationships, and when one of the resident cats has been absent from home because it has gone missing, been at the veterinary surgery or a cattery, it is not uncommon for fur to fly when it comes back into the social group.

Preventing aggression

To minimize the risk of confrontation between cats when introducing a new cat into your home, you must consider the best combination for a multi-cat household. Littermates give the best chance of harmony, and many kittens are inseparable if they stay with each other from birth. Remember that there is a high degree of individual variation and, to some extent, it is believed that sociability, i.e. the desire to form social interactions with other cats, is genetically determined. Certainly some adult cats are more sociable than others and are more tolerant of other cats within a relatively small territory, whilst some are singularly intolerant and give a terrible prognosis for integration.

Gently does it

It helps to have the newcomer in another room for the first few days, where it is out of sight but can infiltrate scent signals into the house. Communal bedding, toys and feeding bowls can be alternated between the resident cat and newcomer. It helps to associate the newcomer's smell with yours – use some items of your clothing, such as sweatshirts.

When introducing cats, protection is important. They have a strong sense of self preservation, and when danger looms their instinct is to run which makes the other cat give chase. This can destroy any hopes of integration but can be avoided by using an indoor pen. Provide escape routes and safe havens for both cats. Shelves and high-up resting places can create extra living space and give them more opportunity to escape from one another. If conflict does occur, it is best to distract the quarrelling cats (with chase objects, stroking or possibly titbits).

Kittens are naturally inquisitive, and will be able to create their own safe havens from unfamiliar or aggressive animals within their home environment.

Aggression towards people

Aggression from cats towards their owners is obviously an area of concern and, as with any feline behaviour problem, it is very important to uncover the cat's motivation for the aggression before you attempt to deal with it.

must know

Defensive aggression
If your cat is aggressive towards people because he is fearful, you must be patient and respectful. Do not attempt to punish him as it will only confirm his fears and reinforce the behaviour. Your cat's instinct is to run away from people or things he perceives as dangerous and you must find a valuable reward to motivate him to stick around and not flee.

Reasons for aggression

Aggression can commonly occur as a defence strategy in a cat who is fearful of people, or it may even develop as a misdirected form of predatory behaviour in cats who have limited access to outdoors or are incompetent hunters in search of more readily targeted prey.

Petting and biting syndrome

Another form of aggression from cats towards their owners is the so-called petting and biting syndrome – perhaps one of the most difficult behaviour problems for owners to come to terms with. Not only are the attacks unexpected and unprovoked but they are also deeply distressing since they happen when the owner is petting the cat and showing him love and affection. Often the cat has been sitting happily with the owner for some time when he suddenly turns and bites the hand that strokes him. For most cat owners, such behaviour is totally incomprehensible and they find themselves feeling uneasy when their pet comes for a cuddle. The trust between cat and owner can be severely threatened and, as the owner begins to reduce the periods of interaction for fear of being attacked, the problem actually becomes self-perpetuating.

Inner conflict

Various theories have been put forward to explain this behaviour, but it is now generally accepted that the root of the problem is a conflict between the relaxed and somewhat juvenile cat, who is willing to accept intimate interaction from his owner, and the independent self-determining adult, who feels threatened by the confinement of close contact. This conflict is perfectly normal and most cat owners will recognize that there is a limit to the amount of handling that their pet will accept.

Low tolerance threshold

For some cats, the tolerance threshold is very low, and although the cat starts off by being comforted by the physical interaction from their owner, there comes a point when he develops from a kitten to an adult cat and becomes aware of the implications of such a vulnerable position on his potential for survival as a solitary hunter.

Displacement grooming

The cat's ultimate goal is escape rather than injury. However, the aggression can be very intense; typically, the cat will lash out at his owner with his teeth and claws. As soon as the form of restraint is removed, the cat will usually run a short distance away before pausing to groom. Many owners will find this part of the process somewhat bizarre. The explanation is that the cat first gets away from the potentially threatening situation and establishes a safe flight distance, but then he reacts to this state of inner conflict and confusion by displacement grooming in an attempt to relax and calm down.

Kittens need lots of opportunities to interact with people, but their play needs to be appropriate and they should not be encouraged to hurt human flesh.

The way in which young kittens are handled can have a profound effect on their future behaviour.

Control rather than cure

The aim of therapy is to increase the threshold of reaction at which the inner conflict occurs, and this is achieved by a gradual desensitization. Start by restricting your physical interaction with your pet to a level that he finds totally unchallenging. This starting point will vary between individuals and according to the severity of the problem.

Cats who will sit on their owner's lap for a long time before reaching their point of conflict can begin treatment at the stage where they are fussed on the lap. Individuals for whom the threshold of conflict is particularly low need to go one step back, and you should concentrate on accustoming the cat to a surreptitious stroke along his back while standing on the ground. Any stroking at this stage must be gentle and on the least sensitive parts of the body, such as the back and head. Areas like the stomach and legs should be left until last, and it is important that you do not physically restrain the cat as he needs to know that he can escape at any time.

Once physical interaction is accepted, you can begin putting your cat on your lap, but the secret is to gradually increase the length of time that the cat stays there whilst keeping one step ahead of him and learning to predict when the point of conflict is getting close. You can then terminate any sessions of interaction before the cat has the opportunity to flip into the aggressive response.

Most cats give some warning signals if an attack is imminent. Some of these may be obvious, like restlessness, tail lashing and pupil dilation, but others are more obscure and you will need a lot of practice in learning how to recognize them.

Indoor toileting

Cats are fastidious and like to keep their core territory clean, but depositing urine and faeces in the house is a common behaviour problem, and while some cats may use these deposits as scent markers, others are simply toileting in inappropriate locations.

Reasons for the behaviour

In some cases the cat may not have learned an appropriate association between the garden or litter tray and the act of elimination, but in most cases, house-training has been successfully completed but subsequently broken down. To determine why the usual litter facilities have become unacceptable, look not only at what the litter tray has to offer but also the features of the inappropriate location that make it more attractive as a suitable latrine.

Surface

The surface on which the cat is expected to eliminate is very important in selecting a latrine, and it is well documented that cats prefer soft, rakeable materials when they are digging their hole for elimination. However, owners often find these fine litter types heavy to carry and opt for lighter wooden pellets or newspaper blocks, and these can cause problems for some cats. These litters are often uncomfortable underfoot, and for indoor cats with soft, sensitive pads, a hard litter can lead to avoiding the litter tray and selecting the carpet as an alternative substrate. The carpet is soft and comfortable and before long the cat develops a strong association with this surface and toilets on it in preference to any other substrate.

must know

Identifying the cause
The reason why a cat feels the need to toilet away from his litter tray needs to be determined before you start any treatment. Compiling an accurate history is the first step to unravelling the mystery. You must find out whether the cat is using the tray or going into the garden to relieve himself. This may indicate the level of aversion to the provided facilities versus the level of attraction to the new location.

Location

The position of toileting facilities is very important to cats, and when their owners place litter trays in unacceptable locations they have no choice but to move away to a more suitable spot. Cats are renowned for their hygienic nature and yet many owners still position litter trays next to feed bowls and expect their cats to use the facilities. Since it is the owner who determines where food is given, the cat can only increase the distance between his kitchen and bathroom by changing his toileting site.

Quiet and seclusion

As well as keeping food and excreta separate, most cats will usually select the most quiet and secluded locations to go to the toilet. Owners need to do their best to mimic the locations that cats would naturally choose for their litter tray. Trays that are positioned next to the dog's bed, right beside the cat flap, under the stairs and in busy traffic areas within the house are unlikely to be considered acceptable by a species that naturally turns its back on the world at this most private of moments.

Cats need privacy, and owners should be careful to ensure that efforts to encourage the cat to use a tray don't backfire.

Treating the problem

Simple alterations to litter type and tray location can often be sufficient to make the litter tray attractive once more, but in view of the long-standing nature of most of these toileting problems it will also be necessary to consider the attractiveness of the unsuitable latrine location and to work to make it less appealing. One of the main attractions in terms of latrines for cats is smell – cats are encouraged back to areas by the residual smell of previous deposits. It is important to clean the soiled areas effectively, using the same regime as the one described for marking deposits (see page 115), and to redefine the function of the location as one that is incompatible with toileting.

Territorial zones

Cats will divide their territory into zones, and the inner core territory is the place where a cat will eat, sleep and play. For the domestic cat, our aim is for the house to be interpreted as the core territory. Ensuring that appropriate activities are available on a regular and predictable basis within the home will help in this interpretation. Toileting usually occurs at the boundary between the core and the home areas, and therefore placing litter facilities at the periphery of the home should be beneficial.

Improving the litter facilities and discouraging the use of any alternative sites are the main aims of treatment for feline toileting problems. In many cases, a purely behavioural approach may be entirely successful in reforming the behaviour. However, life is not always simple and some cases of inappropriate toileting can be frustratingly difficult to resolve. Ruling out any potential medical causes of the accidents is essential for treating the behaviour effectively in these cases, and if the cat is found to be in good physical health a behavioural consultation will offer you the best opportunity of getting to the root of the problem through taking an accurate and detailed history.

Kittens need opportunities to play with appropriate litter substrates from a very early age.

must know

Multi-cat homes
Ideally, in multi-cat households there should be one litter tray per cat plus one extra. Cats do not like to share or to queue up to use the bathroom. If your cat urinates or defecates in the wrong place, you could try placing the litter tray right on the spot he's picked. When he starts using the tray, you can move it to a more appropriate area.

Scratching the furniture

Scratching is a complex behaviour and it has both functional and marking components. The marking of a cat's territory involves the deposition of both a visual and a scent signal, and treatment for this has already been discussed (see page 114).

It is very important to determine whether indoor scratching is a functional or marking behaviour.

Solving the problem

There are times when cats scratch within the home in a functional manner – scratching the furniture to keep their claws in shape – and in these cases, you need to redirect the normal behaviour onto an acceptable surface. The new material should be placed directly onto or in front of the affected area and, once the cat has begun to use it, it can be moved gradually to a more acceptable location.

Commercially available scratching posts provide a convenient way of catering for the cat's scratching needs, but they must be sufficiently high, since the cat needs to be able to scratch at full stretch in order to adequately exercise his clawing apparatus.

Claw trimming

Trimming the claws regularly may be considered, especially if the cat is kept totally indoors and is reluctant to use a scratching post, but it does not affect the actual scratching behaviour and merely limits the damage. In North America, removing the claws by a surgical procedure called declawing is advocated by some veterinary surgeons, but it is not considered acceptable practice by British vets and therefore it is not used in the United Kingdom.

Eating houseplants

One form of unusual appetite that is very commonly reported in cats is that of plant or grass eating, and while the ingestion of plant material may not be natural for a carnivore there are a number of theories as to why this behaviour may develop. However, no owner wants their cat to eat their houseplants.

Why do cats eat plants?

It may be that vegetable matter is consumed as a good source of roughage or that it provides certain minerals and vitamins that are not available in other foods. However, this seems less likely nowadays in the age of good-quality proprietary pet foods.

Another possible explanation is that the plant material has some emetic properties and assists the cat in bringing up hair balls from the digestive tract; this is quite a feasible option.

Preventing the behaviour

Whatever the motivation for this rather bizarre behaviour, many cat owners find it very frustrating to have their precious house plants nibbled at the edges, and in order to avoid this happening it is sensible to provide indoor cats with the trays of seedling grass sprouts which are grown specifically for this purpose and which are sold specially for cats in many pet shops.

Most cats find these grass sprouts more attractive than the average houseplant, and even when they do have access to outdoors, they have been known to wait until they get back into the house to have a nibble on their own special grass.

It is common for some inquisitive kittens to show an interest in houseplants, but for some this interest will develop into an appetite for plant material.

Over-grooming

Grooming is important for keeping the cat's coat in condition, in cat-to-cat communication, maintaining the stability of feline social groups, and regulating stress and conflict by stimulating the release of internal calming chemicals.

A range of stress factors in the cat's environment can lead to problems of over-grooming, including fear and anxiety.

Displacement activity

Grooming as a calming technique is a displacement activity and this can become excessive and lead to hair loss, skin damage and even self-mutilation. Cats can remove quite large quantities of hair, often from their flanks, medial thighs and tail area, in a relatively short space of time. Any cat who loses hair over his body or shows signs of skin damage needs to be examined by a vet before concentrating on potential behavioural causes for the problem.

Treatment

Treatment involves boosting the cat's confidence as well as identifying the trigger for the behaviour and limiting or preventing exposure to it. In some cases, the cause may not be something that can be readily removed from his environment, such as a newborn baby or the next-door dog, and the cat needs to develop other ways of relieving stress. By providing opportunities for him to use other less damaging coping strategies, such as hiding on high-up resting places, you can limit the level of over-grooming. One of the potential side effects is the formation of hair balls in the digestive tract. In extreme cases, surgery is needed to remove these, so grooming anxious or fearful longhairs is an absolute priority.

Abnormal feline appetites

The existence of a depraved appetite leading to the ingestion of non-nutritional substances is called 'pica', and cats have been reported to eat a wide variety of non-nutritional items, including wool, cotton, synthetics, paper, card and even rubber.

Unsuitable substances

Cats can chew or eat these substances, and ingesting unsuitable materials can lead to an obstruction of the intestinal tract. In extreme situations, surgery may even be required. However, cats can take in phenomenal volumes of fabric over their lifetime without experiencing obvious problems. The most common age to start to display this bizarre behaviour is between two and four months. The stress of moving from the breeder to their new home could be a trigger, but some kittens may be born with a genetic predisposition to these abnormal appetites.

Treating the condition

Preventing access to inappropriate material may seem to be the ideal solution but can be difficult.

- Increase the opportunity for hunting-related play by providing appropriate toys and food substances.
- Increase the amount of time that the cat spends in locating and preparing his food.
- Provide food that requires the cat to chew, such as cooked meat-covered bones.
- Hide food around the home to increase the time that the cat has to spend searching for his food.
- Decrease the attraction of the target material by applying taste deterrents.

must know

Negative associations
Owner-associated punishment of any form is never appropriate. The cat will form a negative association with eating wool or fabric in the owner's presence and will become a secret wool eater, which will be far more difficult to treat.

Straying and leaving home

It is said that we do not own our cats, and when they have free access to the great outdoors there is no guarantee they will stay with us. Cats are more in charge of their own existence than our canine companions, and when pressure gets too great within a household, then moving out can become a viable option.

must know

A new home
When you move house with your cat, it will take some time for him to adapt to his new surroundings, but with repeated excursions into the garden and returns to the house for feeding, he should rapidly learn that this new house is now home and he is less likely to stray or to try and find his old home.

Why do cats stray?

Common situations that sometimes cause cats to leave home and move on include the following:
- The arrival of a new cat, dog or human in the existing household.
- Problems of integration in the neighbourhood.
- Attraction back to a previous home following a house move by the owners.

Preventing the behaviour

Most owners wish to minimize the risks of losing their pets, and some people go to the extreme of always keeping their pet indoors in order to avoid problems of straying and leaving home. However, this is not the only approach that is available to owners. Cats are strongly bonded to their territory,

Providing a good supply of palatable food, together with warmth, play and human interaction, should help to identify the house as home.

and while they may not have a great motivation to be loyal to their owners, they will usually stay close to their territory. It is possible to increase this bond to your house and garden by ensuring that only positive associations are made. You can do this by providing valuable resources, and also by working to ensure that food, shelter, affection and privacy are available in abundant supply. This will help to maintain the cat's interest in his home.

Do not be overpowering

It is important not to be too overpowering when you are interacting with cats. Too much human intervention in the form of oppressive affection and high levels of owner-initiated contact can have the opposite effect and actually increase the likelihood of cats moving out. Adopting a far more offhand attitude, which leaves the cat asking for more of your company, will be a far more effective strategy.

Moving house

When you are moving house, remember that cats are likely to want to return to their old territory, and when the two properties are close together it is not unusual for the cat to regularly return to his previous garden.

The risks of this behaviour can be reduced by ensuring that your cat has a high concentration of his own scent within his new home. You can maximize this by confining the cat to barracks for the first couple of weeks after you move house. By releasing him into the garden just before his usual feeding time you can increase his motivation to stay close to your new home.

want to know more?

• Free information on a wide range of behaviour problems and how to remedy them can be accessed at The Blue Cross website on: www.bluecross.org.uk

weblinks

• To find a pet behaviour counsellor in your area, you can email The Association of Pet Behaviour Counsellors: apbc@petbcent.demon.co.uk or you can look on their website at: www.apbc.org.uk

5 Healthcare

Care and consideration for your cat are more than an expression of love; they are a rewarding investment bringing many tangible benefits for both of you. Some simple preventive measures can help to ensure a longer, happier life, better condition and improved fitness for your cat. However, sickness and accidents do occur, even in the most careful households, so you need to be able to recognize the warning signs and know what to do if your cat becomes unwell.

The healthy cat

The health problems that can afflict cats are being increasingly researched, and we now know quite a lot about both how similar and how different cats are compared to dogs or humans when they are unwell, injured or in trouble.

What you can do

The main aim in this section of the book will be to explain a range of different symptoms and what you should do about them, together with some simple, useful first-aid, with the emphasis on the 'first'. You must always seek veterinary help as soon as

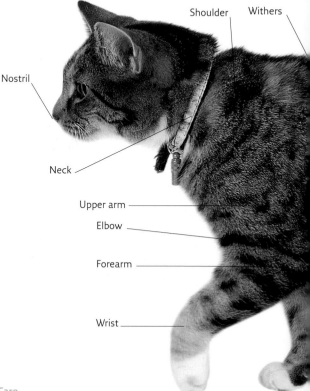

Shoulder Withers

Nostril

Neck

Upper arm

Elbow

Forearm

Wrist

possible for all but the mildest medical conditions. The basic principles behind some of the most common diseases of cats will be described, together with the various ways in which the veterinary surgeon can counter-attack these afflictions.

Prevention is better than cure

Prevention always being better than cure, make sure that your cat is vaccinated against the major feline diseases (see pages 50 and 149) and receives regular boosters. Examine him regularly to check that his behaviour, movements and posture are all normal; that eating and drinking are as usual; and that the mouth, ears, eyes and anus are clear and clean.

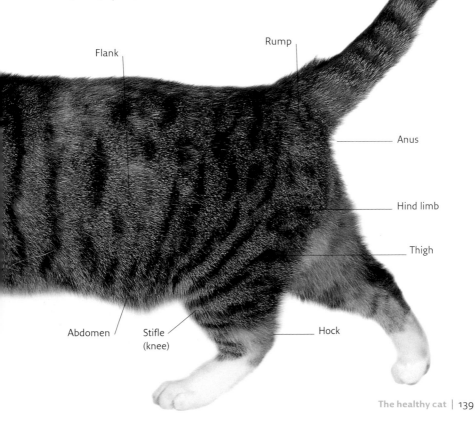

Flank

Rump

Anus

Hind limb

Thigh

Abdomen

Stifle (knee)

Hock

The good owner
Your cat's daily health is your responsibility and, as a good owner, you should try to keep him free of disease. Regular worming, vaccinations, flea control and teeth cleaning will all be necessary. And if your cat is allowed to roam freely outside, he will have to be neutered. This will help prevent him getting into fights with other cats or going astray and leaving home.

Health problems

In this section of the book, we shall begin with the cat's head and look at his mouth and the health problems that can afflict this area of his body. After the mouth we shall travel from head to tail through the various systems of the feline body.

Recognizing the warning signs

If you, the owner, look after your cat properly, take time to groom him regularly – especially if he is a longhair – and feed him a high-quality, nutritious diet, then you will help to prevent many of the common diseases and health problems that can affect cats. It is also a good idea to check your cat regularly for the warning signs of potential illness or poor health. By recognizing them in the early stages, you can prevent many occurring or, at least, treat them before they become serious. You should also ensure that your cat is vaccinated against the principal infectious diseases. Ask your veterinary surgeon for advice on this.

A well-fed cat who is regularly groomed and gets sufficient play sessions and exercise is more likely to stay fit and healthy.

Mouth problems

This sharp end of the cat should be inspected regularly. Cleaning the teeth with a soft toothbrush using salt water or toothpaste specially designed for pets will stop the build-up of plaque and tartar. It will save untold problems for the older cat in years to come if you spend just a few moments now on this easy job.

Tartar and infections

If tartar, a yellow to brown, cement-like substance, accumulates to any extent, it does not produce holes in the teeth that might need filling. Instead, it damages the gum edge, lets bacteria in to infect the tooth socket and thereby loosens teeth.

Chronic infections in the tooth surroundings can lead to serious disease in distant parts of the body, such as the kidneys or heart. There is always some degree of gum inflammation (gingivitis) with tartar and usually an unpleasant smell.

Common symptoms

These include salivating (slavering), pawing at the mouth, exaggerated chewing motions and tentative chewing as if dealing with a hot potato.

What to look for

Open the cat's mouth and look for a foreign body stuck between the teeth. A piece of bone often wedges between the teeth and against the roof of the mouth. Fish-bone pieces sometimes lodge between two adjacent molars at the back of the mouth. You can probably flick a foreign body out with a teaspoon handle or a similar instrument.

must know

Feline dentistry
Your vet has all the specialist equipment and expertise to attend to mouth matters. If many teeth have to be removed from an elderly cat, do not worry. Foods, such as minced, cooked liver, poached fish, cereals with milk and the 'in-gravy' sort of canned cat food, are all easily ingested, even by toothless veterans. No teeth at all is better than having septic gums and rotten teeth that create misery and can poison the cat's system.

If there is no foreign body
If you can't find a foreign body, look for any smooth, red, ulcerated areas on the tongue. These can be the result of licking an irritant substance but they are more commonly caused by the viruses that are associated with feline influenza (see page 148) and sometimes those causing feline infectious enteritis (see page 153), feline infectious anaemia (see page 164) and possibly feline leukaemia (see page 164).

Mouth ulcers

If your cat develops mouth ulcers, you should get veterinary help as soon as possible, since a course of antibiotic injections may be needed to prevent secondary infection. Ulcers can often result from a Vitamin B deficiency, and nicotinic acid tablets may be prescribed where this is suspected.

Common symptoms
The symptoms of mouth ulcers include profuse slavering, unwillingness to eat and general dullness.

Toothache

Diseased teeth may often be a cause of toothache. To check whether your cat has any loose, diseased teeth, open his mouth and touch each tooth very gently with your finger or a pencil. Look out for any wobbling of the tooth or some sign of pain. Do not give your cat aspirin to relieve suspected toothache; aspirin is poisonous to cats. Take him to the vet.

Common symptoms
When your cat has toothache, he may well paw at his mouth or chew excessively.

Tongue or lip swellings

A swelling that appears quite rapidly under one or both sides of the tongue is called a ranula. It is not a tumour or cyst, nor is it serious. Ranulas usually arise because of the blockage of a salivary duct. Your veterinary surgeon can successfully treat the condition if it afflicts your cat, either under sedation or light anaesthetic.

A chronic swelling, which is often topped by an open sore or an ulcer on a cat's lip, may be an eosinophilic granuloma, which is commonly called a 'rodent ulcer'. True rodent ulcers in human beings are cancerous tumours. Occasionally this is also the case in the cat, but most of them are not tumours.

The cause of eosinophilic granulomas is still not fully understood. Whereas some may be due to bacterial, particularly staphylococcal, infection, in other cases, abrasion by a rough tongue or fang tooth, virus disease or autoimmune disease has been implicated.

Common symptoms

The symptoms will include translucent 'cyst-like' swelling under one or both sides of the animal's tongue, difficulty in eating, and swollen, sore or ulcerated lips.

What you can do

Applying creams or ointments to 'rodent ulcers' is always problematical. The medication is usually quickly licked off by the cat and a dressing is impossible. Systemic treatment by means of oral preparation or injections or other forms of physical treatment are indicated. Ask your vet.

must know

Wild cats
Unlike their domestic cousins, wild cats rarely experience dental problems due to their diet of eating the raw flesh, muscle and bones of their prey. Skin and muscle tissues physically clean the tooth enamel. Even if your cat roams around freely outside and catches the odd mouse or bird, he is unlikely to be hungry enough to eat it, bones and all. He will prefer the meals that you put down for him to eat.

Eye problems

For many owners, one of the cat's most attractive features is its eyes with their vertically slit pupils and large coloured irises. Check your pet's eyes regularly to make sure they are healthy.

Soreness and inflammation

If one, or both, of your cat's eyes is obviously sore and inflamed, or if the eyelids are swollen, then an infection, wounding or foreign bodies, such as grass awns, may be involved.

Common symptoms
The cat's eyes may look red or be sore or runny with discharge and matter in the surrounding fur. There may be a blue or white film over the eyes.

What you can do
If the cat is not very concerned, you can drop some Golden Eye liquid (available from the pharmacist) into the affected eye – you need to use one drop, applied three times daily. For more troublesome or persistent cases, consult your vet.

An alternative is to apply Golden Eye or similar ointment. However, this is usually a job requiring two people as the cat may resist you. One person holds the cat while the other gently steadies the animal's head and, with the nozzle of the eye ointment tube parallel to the eyeball, not pointing at it, squeezes out about 1 cm ($^1/_2$ in) of the ointment so that it falls between the eyelids onto the cornea. The eyelids should then be held closed for a few seconds to let the ointment melt.

Third eyelid

The partial covering of the eye by the third eyelid is a common and curious phenomenon, and it often happens in otherwise apparently healthy cats. It can be a result of weight loss, when the eye sinks back as the fat padding within the eye socket is reduced, or it may be an early symptom of feline influenza. Don't worry; the cat isn't going blind, but you must keep a careful watch on the creature.

Common symptoms

The protrusion of a white skin (the haw, third eyelid or nictitating membrane) over some or most of one or both eyes from the inner corner.

What you can do

Should other symptoms develop, see your vet. If it persists for long without other signs, try boosting your cat's food intake and give him 50 micrograms of vitamin B12 daily in his food or as a tablet.

Veterinary treatment

Your vet will have a number of ways of dealing with the varieties of eye disease: using local anaesthetic drops to numb the eye for the removal of irritant objects; or applying drugs, not just by using ointment and drops but also by an injection under the conjunctiva, the pink membrane round the eye. He can also examine deep into the cat's eye with his ophthalmoscope and can identify infecting bacteria by taking swabs of the cat's tears.

Nowadays the vet can even deal with a squint, blocked tear ducts, cataractous lenses and many other eye conditions by surgery.

must know

Genetic disorders
A gene present in some Siamese cats produces faulty 'circuitry' in the optic nerve connecting the eye to the brain. The effect of this is to reduce the cat's binocular vision and give rise to some degree of double vision, making the cat squint as he tries to merge the duplicate images.

Ear and nose problems

Like every other part of your cat's anatomy, it is very important to check the ears and nose regularly in order to identify any potential health problems and prevent them becoming worse.

Ear problems

If your cat starts shaking his head and scratching his ears, check out the problem immediately. It may be due to one of many common complaints.

Common symptoms
These include shaking and tilting the head to one side, scratching the ears, ballooning of an ear flap, tiny white 'insects' inside the ear, and a smelly or chocolate coloured discharge.

What you can do
If ear trouble flares up suddenly, pour in paraffin oil, warmed to body heat. Do it in the garage – puss will flick out any excess oil. If he is an ear-flicker and the ears seem dry but contain white 'insects' (otodectic mange mites), use ear mange drops from the vet.

Veterinary treatment
Any discharge constitutes canker and may need antibiotic treatment by the vet. Head-tilting and loss of balance may indicate Otitis Media (middle ear disease). This is inflammation behind the ear-drum in the middle ear, often following throat and respiratory infections. It needs immediate veterinary treatment to prevent permanent damage to the ear and the spread of infection to the brain.

Haematoma

This big blood blister is due to bleeding within the ear flap, usually caused by vigorous scratching or a blow or a bite from another animal. It is not painful unless it is secondarily infected.

Common symptoms

The ear flap balloons and the cat shakes his head, trying to dislodge the weight. Left untreated, the blood inside the haematoma clots and shrinks into a scar, crumpling the ear into a 'cauliflower' shape.

Veterinary treatment

Under general anaesthetic, the vet can drain off the blood and then stitch the ear in a special way. The success rate is high, but the cause of the original scratching (mites, canker, etc.) must be treated simultaneously.

Nose problems

The appearance of similar symptoms to those of the common cold may signify feline influenza. Even after recovery, many cats remain snuffly and catarrhal for several months or even years.

Common symptoms

These include running, mattery nostrils, snuffling and sneezing.

What you can do

Bathe the delicate nose tip with warm water. Soften and remove any caked mucus and then anoint with petroleum jelly. Feline influenza needs veterinary attention so seek professional advice immediately.

must know

Keep ears clean
You can help prevent ear infections by inspecting your cat's ears every week and cleaning them out, if necessary, with a little olive oil on a soft cotton wool ball. Never use cotton wool sticks in your cat's ears. If you notice anything unusual ring the vet's surgery.

You can use some ear-cleaning fluid to gently clean the ears.

Respiratory problems

Cats can suffer from bronchitis, pneumonia, fluid build-up in the chest cavity, including pleurisy, and other chest conditions. Coughing and sneezing – the miserable signs of a human head cold – perhaps accompanied by eye or nasal discharge, may be the tell-tale signs of feline influenza (cat 'flu).

must know

Other problems
Laboured breathing in a cat without any 'cold' symptoms may be a sign of pleurisy or even of heart disease in older animals. If in doubt, take him to the vet and get him checked out as soon as possible.

Feline influenza

This is usually caused by a mixture of viruses and secondary germs. The most important of the 'flu viruses are those of feline rhinotracheitis and feline calicivirus. Feline influenza may be mild or severe and sometimes ends fatally. In such cases, the damage may be done by secondary bacterial lung infections. It is not a cold, wet-weather disease, and many outbreaks occur in summer.

Common symptoms

These include coughing and sneezing, gasping and laboured breathing in the affected cat.

What you can do

Protect your cat against feline influenza by ensuring that he is vaccinated regularly. There is no connection between the human and cat forms of 'flu. Keep a cat with chest trouble warm and dry, and do not let him exert himself. Give him nutritious food, finely minced or in liquid form, if he will accept it. Keep the nostrils unblocked if possible by sponging the nose and greasing it with petroleum jelly. In cases where the cat continues to eat and his breathing is not too distressed, cough mixture may be given.

Veterinary treatment

More serious cases of feline influenza will have
to be treated by the vet using antibiotics, drugs
to loosen mucus in the lungs and, where the heart
is involved, special cardiac medicines. Where fluid
does accumulate in the chest in pleurisy cases,
the vet may tap this off under sedation. Very many
cats with dicky hearts can now live happy, long
lives once their problem has been diagnosed and
a maintenance treatment has been prescribed.

Vaccination

A primary course of vaccination begins at eight to
nine weeks of age with one injection followed by
a second three to four weeks later. Some vaccines
also protect against other cat diseases. Booster
doses of the vaccine are best given annually.

Feline chlamydial infection

This is an ailment whose signs can resemble those
of feline influenza. Eye inflammation and discharge
are often pronounced. The cause is a germ, which
is not a virus, called *Chlamydia psittaci*, which is
closely related to the one that is found in parrots
(psittacosis) and another that has killed a large
number of koala bears.

Veterinary treatment

The germ can be treated by your vet who may use
antibiotics, such as tetracyclines and erythromycin.
A vaccine is also available and this, too, can be given
from nine weeks of age onwards, either alone or in
combination with the vaccines for feline influenza
and feline enteritis.

Tummy troubles

Cats can be afflicted by many tummy problems, which may be caused by a wide range of factors, including poor diet, nutritional deficiencies, fur balls and ingesting poisonous substances.

Vomiting

This may be transient, due to a mild inflammation (gastritis) of the stomach or the presence, especially in longhairs, of a fur ball. If severe, persistent or accompanied by other major signs, it can indicate more serious conditions, such as feline infectious enteritis, tumours or intestinal obstruction.

Gastritis

Pure gastritis is not common and is generally caused by the ingestion of poisons or irritant chemicals.

Fur balls

These are very common. As a cat grooms himself, he swallows hairs which gradually build up into a soggy mass which, when regurgitated, is frequently sausage shaped. If the fur ball is not vomited out, it grows ever larger, producing erratic appetite and eventually weight loss and poor condition in the cat.

Diarrhoea

This may be relatively simple – the result of too much liver or too many yeast tablets or a mild bowel infection. However, it may be more serious and profuse, as in cases of feline infectious enteritis, feline infectious peritonitis or bacterial infections, including Salmonellosis. Seek advice from your vet.

Constipation

This may be a result of old age, the accumulation of fur balls in the intestine or a faulty diet, or it may even be an indicator of obstruction.

Blood in the stools

This may be merely from the scratching of the intestinal lining by gobbled bone splinters, or it can be the effect of an acute food-poisoning attack.

Bad breath

Bad breath in cats can result from mouth infections, such as gum ulcers and tooth decay, etc., or from digestive upsets or Vitamin B deficiency.

Excessive thirst

This may indicate the presence of a significant disease, such as diabetes, kidney or liver problems, hormonal upsets, uterine disease (including pyometra) or certain toxic conditions.

Overeating

Overeating may be quite normal when a cat is recovering from an illness or after giving birth, but it can also indicate the presence of parasites, diabetes, pancreatitis or hormonal disease.

Lack of appetite

Poor appetite can result from a variety of disorders, ranging from the mild to the serious. Flatulence may be of dietary origin or may indicate intestinal problems, such as the faulty absorption of nutriments (malabsorption).

must know

Treating vomiting
Where vomiting is the prime symptom, do not give your cat any solid food but concentrate on liquid replacement. Persevere if vomiting continues. Do not use milk or brandy. Half a teaspoonful of Maalox or baby gripe water can be given. If the vomiting persists in spite of your efforts, seek veterinary advice without delay.

Cats will drink from many sources but if you think that your cat is drinking excessively, this may be a symptom of liver or kidney related disease or diabetes.

must know

When to ring the vet
If symptoms persist for more than a few hours or are accompanied by malaise and weakness, you need skilled help. Water and salt loss through vomiting or diarrhoea is the killing factor, and you can do something to combat this. Spoon frequent small quantities of glucose and water, seasoned with table salt, into the cat. Above all, use your common sense when dealing with tummy troubles.

Treating tummy problems

For diarrhoea, concentrate on administering fluid. A teaspoon of Kaopectate mixture can be given by mouth. Do not try human kaoline and morphine diarrhoea mixtures. During the early stages of constipation, spoon 2–3 teaspoonfuls of mineral oil (liquid paraffin) into the cat. The tiny, ready-to-use, disposable enemas, available at the chemist, are very effective. Use a half to one tube, as directed for humans on the instructions. If constipation is a chronic problem, add bulk to the cat's diet in the form of bran flakes or isogel granules.

Severe or persistent cases always need veterinary attention. The vet can examine the alimentary tract of the affected animal in various ways – with his fingers, by X-ray, sometimes with barium meal, by stethoscope, gastroscope, ultra-sound and, occasionally, by an exploratory operation.

Feline infectious enteritis

This virus disease is highly contagious and resistant to many antiseptics. It is not purely a complaint affecting the intestines; it also attacks the liver and white blood cells. It can run a fatal course within a matter of hours after an incubation period of two to nine days. Symptoms include depression, vomiting, diarrhoea (not always present), rapid dehydration, sitting in a 'hunched-up' posture and evidence of a painful abdomen when the cat is handled.

Treatment

The cure is prevention. Have your cat vaccinated at eight weeks of age, with regular boosters. Special vaccines are given to queens to provide antibodies for new-born kittens. Antibiotics may control secondary bacterial attack and will protect the affected animal from dehydrating through fluid loss with saline transfusions, under the skin or intravenously.

Feline infectious peritonitis

This special type of peritonitis is due to a virus that usually strikes cats under three years of age. As well as the peritoneum, the virus invades the liver, brain kidneys, and frequently has a fatal outcome after a few weeks. Symptoms include abdominal swelling, possibly jaundice and breathing problems.

Treatment

No vaccine is yet available, and veterinary treatment is aimed at countering dehydration and secondary bacterial infection, draining off dropsical liquid and supporting the body's organs with vitamins and certain hormones.

must know

Feline immuno deficiency
This virus disease is often called feline Aids or 'faids'. There is no evidence that people can be infected by cats, although the virus is in the same family as the one that causes human Aids. Infected cats can carry the virus, without showing signs, for years. It may be transmitted by bites although close, long-term contact is also thought to be necessary. Diagnosis is confirmed by a blood test.

Nutritional problems

Nowadays, with a multitude of balanced, complete cat foods available widely in canned, semi-moist and dry pelleted forms, nutritional disease is far less common than it used to be.

Vitamin deficiency

A purely lean meat diet can result in Vitamin A and/or Vitamin D deficiency in the cat. Signs of Vitamin A deficiency include poor condition, bone, skin and eye disease, infertility and abortion. Treat with cod liver oil and liver. Vitamin D deficiency causes bone disease and is corrected by cod liver oil supplements and a more balanced feeding regime.

Commercial cat foods contain added Vitamin B to replace vitamins lost during processing. Feeding too much raw fish can produce a deficiency, leading to convulsions or strokes. Too much over-processed food may lead to a deficiency with anaemia, weight loss and convulsions. Treatment is by injections of Vitamin B, oral supplements or yeast or B-complex tablets and correcting the diet.

Mineral deficiency

If a cat's diet is calcium deficient, rickets may occur in the young, and brittle bones in adults. The most common reason is too much lean meat. Milk, fish (including bones) and balanced commercial foods will correct this. Treat with supplements or sterilized bone flour in the food and perhaps, Vitamin D. To supply sufficient iodine, lightly season food with iodized salt or offer multi-vitamin trace element tablets which are formulated for small animals.

Diabetes

Diabetes mellitus ('sugar diabetes') is caused by a fall in the production of the vital hormone insulin by certain cells that lie within the pancreas. It can affect cats as well as us humans.

Susceptible cats

The disease is more common in older fat cats, and some breeding lines have an increased tendency to suffer from it. Diagnosis is confirmed by blood and urine tests carried out by your veterinary surgeon.

What you can do

Treatment is by insulin injections and adjusting the cat's diet. Don't worry; you'll find it easy. Insulin is cheap and can be given by you without upsetting the cat. Your vet will show you how to inject it, usually into the scruff of the neck. Most cats don't feel a thing! The frequency of injections and dosage will vary, according to illness, stress or changes in diet. Be guided by your vet who will show you how to assess progress by using testing strips dipped into a puddle of the cat's urine.

The right diet

The patient's diet will be changed to one that is completely free of carbohydrates (including sugar-containing treats) and cereals. For more detailed advice on what to feed, ask your vet.

Urinary problems

Some cats, especially elderly ones, develop problems with their waterworks. The usual signs to watch out for are thirst, loss of weight, blood in the cat's urine and difficulty passing urine.

must know

Accidents
Frequent urination, not emptying the bladder completely and bouts of recurring cystitis are all problems for elderly cats and may help to explain why they may have 'accidents' in the house after many years of being house-trained. Do not scold your cat but seek help from your vet who may be able to treat the problem.

Acute nephritis

This kidney inflammation is caused by infection or poison. Symptoms include vomiting, inflammation of the mouth, thirst, depression, convulsions and coma. Seek urgent veterinary attention.

Chronic kidney disease

This tends to be more common in old cats. Symptoms include thirst, frequent urination, loss of condition and weight and, ultimately, uraemia (retention of waste products in the blood) with vomiting, inflamed mouth, bad breath, dehydration and anaemia. It can be treated by the vet. Unlike the liver, destroyed areas of kidney tissue can't be replaced by healing processes, so surviving, functioning kidney tissue must be supported. The diet should be low in good-quality protein and rich in carbohydrates. Special 'kidney' diets for cats are available on prescription.

Difficulty passing urine

The lower parts of the urinary tract, the bladder and urethra are the most frequent ones to cause trouble, particularly in males. Cats fed on mainly dry-food diets or taking insufficient water and tom cats castrated very early are more prone to develop 'gravel' in the urine. This deposit of salt crystals in the bladder can eventually block up the urethra (water pipe) of male animals. The cat strains to pass urine and you may mistake the position adopted for one of constipation. When the bladder is over-full and tight as a drum, the cat will be in considerable pain, will resent being handled and may actually turn to look at its hind quarters and spit angrily. You must seek veterinary help immediately.

Blood in the urine

This generally indicates bladder infection (cystitis). This complaint is commoner in females. It, too, requires urgent veterinary treatment.

Loss of weight and thirst

These can be due to kidney disease, particularly in old cats, although they may be a sign of other diseases, including diabetes. You must ensure that your cat has plenty of fresh water available and a good proportion of moist food. Add a little salt to his food to encourage him to drink. Do not have a tom castrated too early – wait until he is at least nine months old. The vet can deal with urinary problems.

Reproductive problems

As the male cat's reproductive system is rarely afflicted by any medical problems, we will concentrate in this section on the reproductive problems experienced by the female cat.

Infertility

Failure to breed in cats can be caused by a variety of factors. The ovaries may be inactive with resultant absence of sexual cycling, or they may be overactive through the presence of cysts. Parts of the genital system may be in an abnormal state, as in the case of blocked fallopian tubes. Disease, such as an infection of the uterus or vagina or pyometra, may be grumbling away but showing few symptoms. Veterinary diagnosis can sort out these problems.

Miscarriage

Premature onset of labour is not common but it sometimes occurs. A pregnant queen may begin to strain and bear down even though birth is still a long way off. There may be a discharge from the vulva and the cat may seem dull, unwilling to eat and will sometimes vomit. If you are sure these events are premature, seek veterinary assistance. If you think the queen may well be around 60 days pregnant, wait three hours and then contact the vet if no kitten has been born.

Metritis

Infection of the uterus can follow a birth, especially in older queens or ones who are out of condition for some reason, perhaps after the birth of a dead

kitten, particularly one that has
been delivered by forceps or Caesarean
section, or where all or some of the placenta
has been retained after an otherwise normal
birth. Symptoms are loss of appetite, thirst,
depression, fever, vomiting and discharge of bad-
smelling material from the vulva. Urgent veterinary
attention is needed. Meanwhile, keep the cat warm
and offer warm, nourishing liquids, such as beef tea.

Prolapse of the uterus

Occasionally, following a difficult birth, part or all of
the uterus will balloon out of the vulva as a swollen
red mass. You must seek urgent veterinary help if this
occurs. Meanwhile, you can keep the prolapsed uterus
clean and moist by sponging it gently with a little
cotton wool and warm water before smearing on a
little petroleum jelly and then covering it with a piece
of clean gauze or some cloth.

If the prolapse has not been 'out' for long, your
vet may be able to replace it under sedation or
anaesthetic. However, if some time has elapsed
and the prolapse has swollen markedly or become
infected, an operation may be necessary.

Pyometra

This is not primarily a uterine infection but rather a condition of hormonal origin. Over time, under the influence of an abnormally functioning ovary, changes can occur in the uterine wall with microscopic cysts forming. These lead to inflammation of the walls and the interior of the uterus filling up with a pus-like fluid which eventually poisons the cat.

Common symptoms

The symptoms include a purulent discharge (white, pink, yellow or chocolate) from the vagina, dullness, lack of appetite, thirst and vomiting. This disease is most common in queens who have never had kittens or maybe just one litter. It looks like a septic infection and can make the animal very ill through absorption of the fluid that distends the womb, although in many cases the pus is sterile. It is not an infectious disease although secondary bacterial invasions are a danger.

What you can do

If you are not planning on breeding, have a female spayed when she is young. If discharges are seen, clean the vulval area with warm water and weak antiseptic and take the little lady along to the vet.

Veterinary treatment

The vet may use hormone treatment together with drugs to reduce the amount of fluid in the womb, and antibiotics to tackle any opportunist bugs. The main veterinary weapon is normally a hysterectomy, or the removal of the diseased womb through a side or mid-line incision under general anaesthetic.

must know

Pregnancy
The average pregnancy lasts 63 days. The queen will gain 1–2kg (2–4lb) in weight as her abdomen enlarges. During this time, she will need a high-quality diet with smaller, more frequent meals. She will become quite maternal and about a week before the birth she will start looking for a suitable place to deliver her kittens. Provide a clean box in a quiet, secluded part of your home.

Stopping unwanted pregnancies

Responsible, caring and humane owners take steps to avoid unwanted pregnancies in their cats: toms are castrated and queens spayed. There are other advantages, too: toms stray less, don't get into macho fights on rooftops by moonlight and desist from spraying territory with pungent urine markers. Queens aren't pestered by neighbourhood lotharios, and their owners are spared the love-lorn howling of a female in heat.

Oestrus suppression

If you want your queen to have kittens, but in a controlled fashion, there are other methods of oestrus ('heat') suppression. Injections or tablets can be prescribed by the vet to temporarily postpone (useful at holiday times), permanently postpone, or suppress (if already begun) an oestrus period. These enable a return to normal sexual cycling when desired, but some vets are against using them repeatedly as a replacement for spaying, particularly in queens who have never had kittens. Overuse of hormonal preparations can lead to ovarian or uterine disease in later life. Ask your vet which is the most appropriate regime. The contraceptive pills used in cats can have side effects, such as increased appetite, unwanted weight gain and sluggishness. They cannot normally be given to diabetic animals.

Spaying

This is best performed when your cat is between four and nine months. It can be done from three months onwards to almost any age. Kittens under three months of age and queens in oestrus ('heat') or more than four weeks pregnant must *not* be spayed.

Castration

Toms can be castrated from six months but it is best to wait until they are nine months in order to avoid urinary blockages in the penis in later life.

Circulatory problems

Just like us, cats may suffer from circulatory problems, especially as they grow older. They can also be afflicted by the deadly feline leukaemia, but you can vaccinate them to prevent this.

must know

Heart worms
These afflict cats in the Far East, Australia, USA and southern Europe. They are only seen in the UK in imported cats. The parasites are transmitted in larval form by fleas or mosquitos. They are difficult to treat as dead worms in the circulatory system can cause more trouble than living ones. Prevention involves controlling fleas and mosquitos and keeping pets indoors at night. If you live in a heart worm area, you should seek veterinary advice.

Heart problems

Cat hearts can be afflicted by different conditions. Kittens may be born with congenital defects in the heart walls ('holes in the heart'). Virus and bacterial disease, such as feline influenza, can cause long-lasting damage to heart tissue. Occasionally the heart can be the site of tumours and, in elderly cats, the passing years may bring weakness or a blockage of the heart valves. Over-active thyroid glands may also affect the heart significantly.

Common symptoms
These include laboured or faster-than-normal breathing, tiring quickly and easily 'running out of puff', coughing, wheezing or gasping, and a lilac-blue tinge to the gums. Where one or more persists for more than a day or two, seek veterinary advice.

Veterinary treatment
The vet will examine the cat's heart and may also employ X-rays, ultra-sound, electrocardiography or blood analysis to make a diagnosis. Treatment will depend on the nature of the disease. Weak hearts may be strengthened and their action improved by drugs. Whatever the treatment, old, tiring hearts may benefit from daily administration of 50 milligrams of Vitamin E or wheatgerm oil in the food.

Anaemia

Anaemia is the reduction in the number of red cells circulating in the blood and/or a diminution in the amount of oxygen-carrying haemoglobin in the red cells. If you suspect anaemia, do contact your vet. It may be caused by any one of the following:

• Destruction of red cells by parasites (as in feline infectious anaemia), poisons, bacterial toxins or an immune reaction following a blood transfusion.

• Loss of blood by wounds, chronic bleeding, internal tumours, ulcers or other lesions, by blood-sucking parasite or by ingestion of a chemical, such as warfarin, which inhibits normal blood clotting.

• The absence, reduction in the numbers or the abnormal production of new red cells in the bone marrow caused by acute or chronic infections, tumours, poisons, chronic kidney disease or a diet lacking in certain essential elements.

Veterinary treatment

Your vet will examine the cat and take a blood sample for analysis. Treatment will depend on the type and cause of the anaemia and may include iron supplements, a course of vitamins and even a blood transfusion from a compatible donor cat.

must know

Anaemia symptoms
An anaemic cat may display some or all of the following symptoms:
• Pale mouth and eye membranes (conjunctiva lining the eyelids)
• In severe cases, the affected cat may be breathless, weak, fatigued and restless

Feline infectious anaemia

This is caused by a minute parasite, which, like the malarial parasite in humans, lives inside the cat's red blood cells. It may be there in small numbers and cause few or no apparent ill-effects. However, if it is present in much larger numbers and becomes more virulent (when a cat's resistance is lowered for some reason), it can destroy the cells.

Common symptoms

The infested cat is soon dull, weak and very out-of-condition. It loses weight progressively and the eye membranes and mouth lining become pallid.

Veterinary treatment

A blood sample is analysed to determine the severity and to confirm the presence of parasites. Feline infectious anaemia can be treated with antibiotics, anti-anaemic therapy and, in advanced cases, blood transfusion, which normally assure a favourable prognosis. If it affects cats who are also afflicted with feline leukaemia, the outlook is not good.

Feline leukaemia

Leukaemia is uncontrolled production of white blood cells. These ordinarily serve vital functions: participating in immunity defences against infections. Too many circulating white cells can clog up blood and lymphatic vessels and invade and damage organs.

Feline leukaemia is contagious and spreads from cat to cat by direct contact. The virus is unable to live for long outside the cat's body and can be killed easily by ordinary disinfectants. While some cats are naturally immune, others can carry and transmit

must know

Thrombosis
This is the blocking of an artery or vein by a clot floating in the blood stream. It can have grave effects. Common symptoms are sudden collapse and shock, pain, paralysis (total or partial) of the hind legs, which usually feel cold to the touch, and disappearance of the pulse in the femoral arteries of both hind legs. Seek veterinary attention. The recovery rate is low and some recurrences may occur.

the virus without showing signs of illness. These are dangerous individuals wherever groups of cats are maintained, as in breeding catteries. Once detected (this can be done by blood testing), they should be isolated from other cats or euthanased.

Common symptoms
These include fever, weakness, lethargy, weight loss and anaemia. Other signs are exhibited where the virus has targeted certain organs. Vomiting and/or diarrhoea, together with enlargement of the liver and spleen, may occur in the abdominal form of the disease. Where the kidneys or thymus are involved, urinary problems or laboured breathing and coughing may be seen. Sometimes the eyes are invaded, causing severe inflammation and blindness.

What you can do
Treatment can be attempted by the vet, but there is no cure and it is usually wise to euthanase the cat to prevent transmission to others. If one cat in a house tests positive, all the other cats should be screened to detect any carriers. The disease can be prevented by vaccination at nine weeks, with a second dose given at twelve to thirteen weeks. 'All-in-one' vaccines combining protection against feline leukaemia, feline influenza and feline infectious enteritis are available.

Skin problems and parasites

There are many kinds of skin disease in cats, and they may be parasitic or non-parasitic. Both types are quite common and you should look out for them at your regular grooming sessions.

The traditional and reasonably effective way of removing fleas is with a flea comb, but, unlike anti-flea medications, it is time-consuming and not fool-proof.

Fleas and mites

A single flea on a cat may set up widespread itchy skin irritation as an allergic reaction. Look out for 'insects' or fine black 'coal dust' – the flea droppings among the hairs. Cats can become infected with feline, dog or human fleas. Apart from damaging the skin and causing itching, fleas can carry tapeworm larvae and certain virus diseases. In late summer, orange specks in the fur of the cat's head, ears or between the toes reveal the presence of harvest mites.

What you can do

If you suspect the presence of any skin parasites, such as fleas, lice, ticks or mites, treat the cat with an anti-parasitic aerosol or powder. Other highly effective anti-parasite treatments available from the vet include injections, drops that are absorbed into the body after being applied to the skin, and special preparations for mixing with the animal's food.

As the flea's eggs are dry and not, like those of the louse, cemented to hairs, they drop off the cat's body. Carpets, bedding and furniture can become flea-ridden, so use a veterinary aerosol containing methoprene and permethrin around the house. If applied to carpets and furniture once every seven months, this product prevents re-infestation of your cat by flea eggs hatching in its environment.

Ringworm

A 'ringworm' fungus can cause skin disease. Signs may be insignificant (areas of scaly, powdery skin) or more obvious (small, circular bald areas with wet or crusty edges). Ringworm can be treated by drugs given orally, but you must take care as it can be transferred to humans, so make sure that bedding and litter are burnt and all boxes and utensils are sterilized in a hot, cat-safe disinfectant.

Non-parasitic skin disease

Eczema, dermatitis and weeping sores can be due to bacterial infection, food allergy, sunburn (in white cats), vitamin deficiencies or other nutritional faults, hormonal problems or by coming into contact with irritant chemicals. Itchy thinning of the hair over the trunk with points of oozing, red scabs is one of the commonest skin diseases.

What you can do

Always seek veterinary advice. Where cats have wet sores, clip away the hair around the lesions to open them to the air and aid healing. Do not apply any creams, powders or ointments without veterinary advice – the animal will lick them off and may suffer ill effects. Gently bathe an inflamed area with warm water and weak antiseptic, then dab it dry.

Veterinary treatment is usually very effective. Bacterial infections can be combated by antibiotics. Food allergies can be identified and the food allergen withdrawn. Nutritional deficiencies are corrected by nutritional supplements to a properly balanced diet. Hormonal problems are treated by administering hormones either orally, by injection or by implants.

must know

Ticks
Rural cats may pick up ticks in fields or woods. These blood-sucking parasites swell up as they feed until they resemble, and are the size of, blackcurrants. Don't pull ticks off as their mouth parts may stay buried in the skin and cause abscesses. Apply an anti-parasitic preparation to the tick's body and then wait for it to loosen its attachment.

Internal parasites

The most important and common parasites are found in the cat's gastro-intestinal tract. They are worms and there are three main types of worm – roundworms, tapeworms and flukes.

Roundworms

These live in the intestinal canal and 'share' the food passing through – they do not suck blood. Their eggs are passed out in the cat's stools and pass to other cats either directly or after being ingested by insects, mice or rats which are subsequently eaten by cats. Common symptoms include poor condition, 'pot-belly', diarrhoea or constipation, and anaemia (pale gums and eye membranes).

Whipworms and threadworms

Less commonly, cats may suffer from whipworms or threadworms (types of roundworms but smaller). The eggs and larvae require no intermediate host and can pass directly from cat to cat. The symptoms are weight and condition loss, diarrhoea and anaemia.

Tapeworms

These parasites, with segmented bodies, visible to the naked eye and more dramatic looking, are not as dangerous as roundworms. They live in the cat's intestines and, again, 'share' the digesting food but do not suck the blood. When the segments pass through the cat's anus they appear like white grains of rice which stick to the hairs beneath the tail. Like roundworms, tapeworms can be prevented by worming your kitten or cat regularly.

Guard the cat's eyes and nose with your hand when using an aerosol. Do not spray too close to the skin.

Toxoplasmosis

An important parasite that can affect humans and other animals as well as cats is *Toxoplasma gondii*. Contracted usually by eating some raw meat, this microscopic organism can attack the intestine and organs of the cat's body.

The signs are varied and they can be subtle but diarrhoea is the commonest symptom. The parasite spreads via the cat's stools and sometimes can be picked up by humans. Although rare, this disease is a particular risk to pregnant women as it can be passed on to their unborn babies.

What you can do

If you are pregnant, you should avoid close contact with cats. All cat food should be either a proprietary brand or, if it is prepared at home, well cooked. Change the cat litter daily (always wearing rubber gloves if you are pregnant) and disinfect your cat's litter trays and their surrounds thoroughly.

When you are gardening, always wear gloves to avoid any contact with contaminated soil where cats may have defecated. Diagnosis by blood tests and subsequent treatment with drugs such as sulphonamides or antibiotics can be undertaken by the vet.

must know

Worming drugs
Modern worming drugs are safe and effective and utterly free of the unpleasant side effects that were once common, so you need have no worries about treating your cat. They can be purchased in pet shops, pharmacies and even supermarkets, or you can obtain them from your veterinary surgery. If you are unsure about which preparation is best for your cat, you should consult your vet.

Problems of the nervous system

Just like humans, cats can have disorders that may affect their brain or spinal cord, or the nerves leading from them. If you suspect that anything is wrong, consult your vet immediately.

Encephalitis

Inflammation of the brain can be caused by viruses, bacteria or protozoan parasites via the blood or from nearby tissues, e.g. an infected middle or inner ear. Poisons can also be responsible. Symptoms are dullness, fever, weakness and staggering, paralysis, epilepsy ('fits'), dilated pupils and coma.

What you can do
Consult your vet immediately. Keep the cat in quiet, stimulus-free surroundings. Treatment normally consists of drugs, e.g. antibiotics and corticosteroids.

Epilepsy ('fits')

These attacks usually begin quite abruptly, and the cat will fall over, frothing at the mouth with its body shuddering, its legs paddling and apparently unconscious. Frequently, urine and faeces are voided. After a few minutes the 'fit' stops, again suddenly, the animal becomes calm and shortly regains its feet, looking as if nothing had happened.

The phenomenon looks painful, but the cat does not suffer any pain during an attack. Resembling an 'electrical storm' in the circuitry of the brain tissue, epilepsy can be due to a variety of causes, some obscure and almost impossible to pinpoint. Tumours, head injuries or parasites may be responsible.

What you can do
When a 'fit' occurs, you must immediately reduce all environmental stimuli. Darken the room, cut down any noise from radios, etc., and put a guard around any open fire. Do not touch or stroke the cat – you may only extend the length of time that the 'fit' lasts. Seek veterinary attention straight away.

Myelitis
Inflammation of the spinal cord, myelitis is caused most frequently by bacterial infection spreading from nearby tissues. Many cases originate from deep cat bites to the back (a common site during fights between rival toms). Other possible causes are viruses (e.g. rabies), parasites (e.g. *Toxoplasma*) and certain poisons. Damage to the spinal cord can also be found after accidents and produces similar symptoms: total or partial paralysis of a limb or limbs, and pain and acute tenderness in the back. Seek urgent veterinary attention. Handle your cat very gently and avoid any flexing of the spine when taking him to the veterinary surgery.

Treatment may involve draining the spinal canal and drugs. If the cat is paralysed, the outlook is very gloomy if distinct improvement is not made within one month. If it does occur, full recovery may take several weeks or months longer.

Physiotherapy may aid recovery and will depend on you and how much time and effort you are prepared to dedicate to your cat.

must know

Concussion
Accidental blows to the cat's head may lead to concussion. Usually this is manifested by initial loss of consciousness followed by signs that may include paralysis, staggering or blindness. Luckily, in most cases, such symptoms are temporary, rarely lasting longer than five days. Treatment by the vet may include giving corticosteroid and/or diuretic drugs and vitamin injections.

Good nursing and hygiene are vital in paralytic cases where control is lost – albeit temporarily – of the bowel or bladder.

Local nerve paralysis

Sometimes a nerve supplying one particular part of the cat's body ceases to function and the area becomes paralysed. A limb or the tail is most common as a result of an accident. Unable to feel or control the appendage, the cat drags it about. Soon, friction with the ground will result in abrasions and then ulceration. If veterinary treatment does not result in distinct improvement within one month of the injury, amputation should be considered. This is carried out under general anaesthetic and is not cruel. The animal is not crippled – cats can get about just as well with only three legs or minus a tail.

Injured cats may be in shock. Keep your cat warm by wrapping him in a blanket or whatever is to hand, and take him to the vet immediately.

Musculo-skeletal problems

Cats develop diseases of the bones, joints and muscles far less frequently than their owners or pet dogs. Injuries are the main type of musculo-skeletal disorder, ranging from minor sprains to broken bones and infections resulting from fighting wounds.

Common causes

The causes of limping or swollen limbs include accidental injury, wounds, fracture, bone infection, tumour (not very common) and arthritis, which is rare. Seek veterinary attention without delay. Never give aspirin or human or dog-type analgesics before getting professional advice. Aspirin is toxic to cats.

Arthritis

This will be treated by suitable anti-inflammatory drugs, including members of the cortisone family of chemicals. If you suspect that your cat may be affected, see your veterinary surgeon.

Infected bites

Apart from traumatic damage caused by accidents, a common reason for lameness or a painful, puffy, swollen foot or leg is an infected bite. During a fight, the needle-like teeth of an opponent can penetrate the skin and reach the bone which generally lies closer to the surface of the body than in dogs. Soft tissue infection and/or deeper involvement of the bone quickly develop, but antibiotics from your vet will control the situation. You may be asked to bathe the area several times a day with some warm water containing a little table salt or Epsom salts.

must know

Grumpy old cats
Some elderly cats with osteo-arthritis can become very grumpy, but the pain can be alleviated with drug treatment from your vet. However, do not try out anti-inflammatory medicines on your cat. They are OK for humans, horses and dogs but are toxic to felines.

Elderly cats

Inevitably, time catches up with our cats, and should your pet survive beyond 17 years, he is doing very well indeed. Very few cats reach one score, although the longevity record at present stands at 34 years, as achieved by a tabby queen from Devon.

must know

When the time comes...
In ancient Egypt, folk would shave off their eyebrows as a token of deepest grief if a cat died naturally. If you are fortunate, your cat will die in his sleep when his time comes. However, as a responsible owner, you may have to make the tough decision for him. If a cat is in pain that is not likely to be relieved or the condition is a hopeless one where the cat is obviously unhappy, it is not only false sentimentality but also irresponsible to deny the creature a dignified, peaceful end.

Physical changes

Old cats need special attention and understanding. After years of faithful companionship, it would be a churlish owner who did not give a thought to coping with their feline geriatrics. Venerable cats change physically. They frequently become rather thin and this may be accompanied by a change in appetite with an increased or decreased demand for food. They may become more thirsty. Certainly some of these are the results of a failing liver and kidneys – conditions that, in the absence of other symptoms, are difficult for the vet to treat.

The right diet

If your cat's appetite increases and he drinks more, give extra food at each meal or, better still, more meals daily. High-quality protein food (fish, meat and poultry) and a variety of vegetables and fruit are good for the pussy pensioner. A teaspoonful of lard mixed with the cat's usual food will provide valuable extra calories for an old, lean cat whose intestines can no longer absorb nutriments very efficiently and who no longer carries an insulating layer of subcutaneous fat. Give your elderly cat more water or milk to drink if he wants it; denying the increased thirst would be dangerous.

Fibre is important

Age may bring fussiness, and focusing on high-quality protein food may produce bowel sluggishness and constipation. Oily fish, e.g. canned pilchards, helps the free movement of the bowel but don't offer lots of rich and tasty morsels; your cat needs roughage.

A little paraffin oil mixed with food can be used occasionally as a laxative (two teaspoonfuls once or twice weekly), but not more often as it cuts down the absorption of the vitamins A, D and E.

If your cat will not take fibre in his food in the form of bran or crumbled, toasted wholemeal bread, use a bulk-acting granular laxative daily. An ideal one is made from plant seed husks. Laxatives of this type are usually well accepted by cats, especially when they are mixed with meals. Once swallowed, they absorb liquid, swell and make bulk that stimulates the contraction of the lazy intestine-wall muscles.

Old cats who have infirmities should be discouraged from any risky situations. This one-eyed veteran on a bird table in a tree lacks the stereoscopic vision required to accurately jump down.

Mouth and teeth

In old age, keep a special watch on the cat's mouth. A fondness for soft snacks in a cat's dotage may encourage rapid tartar formation with secondary gum damage, inflamed tooth sockets and loosening teeth. Catch these things early. Septic areas in the mouth and bad teeth contribute to kidney and liver run-down, and general anaesthesia for multiple extractions can be risky in old age, so do not neglect dental hygiene in youth and middle age. Clean the old cat's teeth once or twice weekly with a soft toothbrush or cotton-wool dipped in salt and water.

Leaking and bowel control

Some old warriors lose control of their bowels or water-works on the odd occasion. This may be forgetfulness, but it may be that nerve control of the various valves involved is weakening. If it

The senior citizen cat requires a modified diet with plenty of fibre to prevent tummy troubles.

becomes troublesome, let your vet check over the animal. Cystitis can be a cause of involuntary 'leaking' and should be treated. Lazy bowels may simply need more bulk content (see page 175).

Diseases of old age

Deafness or failing eyesight usually arise gradually, if at all, and the responsible owner should be able to compensate intelligently for them. For example, remember that a deaf cat cannot hear if you are moving furniture, vacuuming the carpet or bringing a strange dog into the room – all potential dangers from the immediate vicinity of which a cat with good hearing will quickly remove itself. With a blind cat, keep his food dishes in the same place and protect him from open fires and similar dangers; try to avoid rearranging familiar furniture.

Making life easier

Although there is no elixir of life available yet for man or his pets, there are now some drugs that your veterinary surgeon may prescribe that can counteract some of the symptoms of old age. One is sulphadiazine, which is claimed to combat senility, lack of lustre, greying of hair and general lack of interest and vitality where such symptoms are due solely to old age. Other drugs include the range of anabolic hormones that encourage tissue building, oppose wastage of bodily protein, speed up the healing processes, and generally increase appetite, alertness and activity. The vet must decide whether your cat is suitable for treatment with any of these compounds. All elderly cats should be checked over by the vet two or three times a year.

must know

Regular grooming
There is a tendency for old cats to lose personal pride when they are past their prime. They either forget or they cannot be bothered to groom themselves. When grooming longhaired cats, watch out for knots which may build up in the coat. You should groom your cat daily with a comb and brush (see page 64).

Nursing a sick cat

In all your pet's ailments, no matter whether they are mild or serious, you will normally have to be prepared to act as a nurse. There are some essential techniques to be learned when it comes to handling a sick cat and administering medication.

Giving a tablet

This is not easy, ever. Crushed tablets mixed with food are usually detected quickly and Puss marches off in high dudgeon, going without a meal rather than take his medicine. The technique is to hold the cat's head, bending it back on the neck until the mouth automatically opens a fraction. You can keep the mouth open by pushing the lips on each side between the teeth with your index finger and thumb. You may need an assistant for this.

Drop the tablet accurately onto the groove at the back of the tongue. Give a quick poke with the index finger of the other hand (or carefully with a pencil if you feel timid), pushing the tablet over the back of the tongue. Close the mouth and then gently rub the cat's throat until he swallows.

Giving liquids

With the same grip on the cat's head and holding it back firmly, liquid medicines can be dropped slowly into the patient's mouth, either with a small spoon or from a dropper. Do not be impatient and flood your pet's mouth with fluid – the cat will only choke, panic and splutter furiously. Again, you may need someone to hold the cat while you do this.

Restraining a cat

1 Wrapping your cat firmly in a blanket or towel is the best way of restraining him if he is distressed or aggressive.

2 If your cat is an escape artist and struggles, hold him on a firm, flat surface in your arms while you grasp all four legs in your hands.

3 To 'scruff' your cat, press down firmly but gently on his rear end on a flat surface and talk reassuringly to him.

4 Cradling your cat in your arms and holding him close to you, is a gentle but effective way of restraining him.

First aid and emergencies

Nine lives or not, when cats get into scrapes, prompt action by you can make all the difference between tragedy and a quick return to normal, so learn some basic first aid techniques.

Emergency action

When an accident occurs, get someone to phone the vet's surgery at once while you give practical first aid. It is usually quicker for you to take the cat to the surgery than to wait for the vet to come to you – speed is often a crucial factor in deciding the outcome. You may need to follow the heart massage instructions (see opposite) or perform artificial respiration (see page 182) to save your cat's life.

1 Get the cat out of danger. Move by slipping a sheet under him to form a hammock that you can carry. It is wisest not to raise the head, other than briefly, to avoid blood, saliva or vomit running down the throat and blocking the windpipe.

2 Do not give the cat anything by mouth, either food or water. Keep him comfortable and warm in a quiet place until you leave for the surgery or the vet arrives. If wished, you can place a hot water bottle, covered with a cloth, next to the cat.

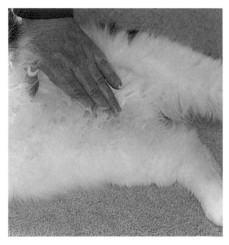

3 You can check the cat's pulse by feeling with your hand on the inside of the thigh as shown before also checking the animal's breathing (see next step).

4 If the breathing is irregular or not apparent, open the mouth, pull the tongue forwards, wipe away any blood and if you can't see it breathing, give artificial respiration (see over).

5 If you cannot detect the pulse on the inner surface of the animal's thigh, you should feel for the heartbeat by placing your fingertips on the chest wall just behind the front leg. Make sure that you try to stay calm and gentle and do not press down too hard.

6 Should the heartbeat be non-apparent, very weak or very slow, then you should give the cat heart massage by rubbing the area over the heart with both hands. Do not be heavy-handed; the cat's ribs can be crushed by the application of too much force.

Artificial respiration

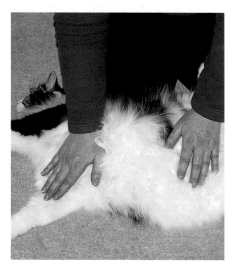

1 Unless there is a possibility that the back or hind legs are injured, swing the cat, head down, by its hind legs like a pendulum to clear away any fluids which may be blocking the cat's airway, by centrifugal force. Grip the cat's feet firmly before starting.

2 If the chest is not damaged, place the palm of your hand on the cat's uppermost ribcage as it lies on its side. Press down at 5-second intervals, releasing the pressure straight away so the chest expands, filling the lungs with air. Do not press too firmly.

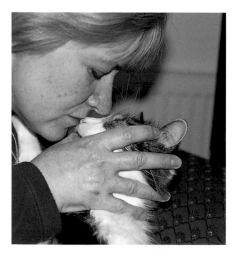

3 With the cat lying horizontally, try 'mouth to nostrils'. Check that the animal's airway is not blocked by fluid, mucus or blood, then apply your lips to the cat's nostrils. Blow in some air steadily for three seconds, pause for two seconds and then repeat.

Note: Rough or too heavy artificial respiration can damage the lungs and heart. Cats are more delicately built than dogs or humans.

Heavy bleeding

Heavy and persistent bleeding must always be staunched. To do this, you must apply firm pressure, preferably over a cotton wool pad, some gauze or even a screwed-up clean paper tissue. Do make sure you maintain the pressure until you get the cat to the vet's surgery. There are pressure points that can be used to stem very severe bleeding (see below).

Dressing a wound

This will apply pressure and keep the area clean but you must take care never to wrap a bandage too tightly around a cat's limb or tail. It is relatively easy inadvertently to form a 'tourniquet', cutting off the blood supply to the animal's extremities with sometimes disastrous consequences. Do not waste any time applying antiseptics, creams or powders to any wound. Seek veterinary attention immediately.

Pressure points

Tail
Press on the artery where it runs along the underside of the tail

Head and neck
Press on the artery in a groove in the lower part of the neck where it meets the shoulder

Fore limb
Press on the artery where it crosses the bone above the inside of the elbow joint

Hind limb
Press on the artery where it crosses over the bone on the inner thigh

must know

Shock
A shocked animal will feel colder than normal and have pallid gums and eye membranes. Don't give alcohol or other stimulants, but keep him warm and seek veterinary assistance without delay.

Burns

These can be caused by extreme cold or electric current, but most commonly result from hot liquids spilled on the cat. Fur does afford a little protection, but nevertheless skin damage, the evidence of which may take some days to develop, is frequent.

What you can do

Apply cold water or ice to the affected area straight away. Then anoint the burn with a greasy ointment, such as petroleum jelly. You must seek veterinary attention even though you may not be able to see any damage to the skin at that time.

Foreign bodies

Sometimes a foreign body can get lodged in your cat's mouth, nose or eye and it will need to be removed, either by yourself or by your vet.

Foreign body in the mouth

Hold the cat firmly to prevent him wriggling and then open the mouth, pushing down the lower jaw with a pencil. You can dislodge the object with your fingers, a teaspoon handle or tweezers.

Foreign body in the nose

Leave it alone. Control the bleeding by applying cold compresses, and seek veterinary help immediately.

Foreign body in the eye

You can try to wash out the foreign body by gently pouring warm (body-heat) water or human-type eye wash into the eye. If the object is not swept out, seek veterinary help.

Common poisons

Chemical	Source	Symptoms
Aspirin	Tablets	Vomiting, liver damage
Lead	Paints (particularly old flaking woodwork)	Nervous signs, paralysis
Ethylene glycol (anti-freeze)	Car radiator drips	Convulsions, wobbliness, depression, coma
Phenols, Cresols, Turpentine, Tar products	Disinfectants (usually ones that turn white when added to water), tar, wood preservatives	Burnt mouth, characteristic smell, vomiting, convulsions, coma
Warfarin	Rodent poisons	Stiffness, haemorrhages, diarrhoea
Arsenic	Horticultural sprays, rodent poisons	Vomiting, diarrhoea, paralysis
Phosphorus, Thallium	Rodent poisons	Vomiting, diarrhoea
Metaldehyde	Slug killer	Incoordination, salivation, rapid breathing, convulsions, coma

Poisons

The house, the garden and the outside world contain many substances that are poisonous to cats. They sometimes ingest toxic substances by eating rodent poison or licking their coat after it has been contaminated with a noxious chemical. Licking puddles of anti-freeze tainted water in the garage is another common cause of poisoning.

What you can do

Where the fur has been contaminated, you can wash the cat in the sink, bath or shower with some human hair or baby shampoo, then rinse and dry the animal thoroughly before contacting the vet.

Washing out poisons

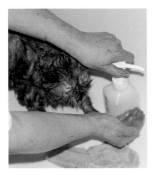

1 Use plenty of human hair shampoo to wash out the poison. Baby shampoo is best for washing around the cat's eyes and face.

2 It is extremely important to shampoo the affected area thoroughly before rinsing out with water. Rub the shampoo in and build up a lather.

3 Rinse away all the traces of shampoo thoroughly; if necessary, repeat the process. Seek professional advice as soon as possible.

Common symptoms of poisoning

Different types of poison will inevitably produce different symptoms in the affected cat. You must watch out for the following signs: vomiting, diarrhoea, wobbliness, stiffness, depression, salivation, haemorrhages, convulsions and even coma.

Note: In all cases of suspected poisoning, there is no time to lose, and seeking professional help is essential. Don't try to diagnose which poison is the culprit unless you know for sure what has affected your cat and can take a sample to the vet for analysis.

want to know more?

• Advice about a wide range of feline health problems can be seen on The Blue Cross website: www.bluecross.org.uk
• To contact the British Veterinary Association, telephone 020 763 66541

weblinks

• For information on toxoplasmosis, log on to: www.womens-health. co.uk
www.nhsdirect.nhs.uk

Need to know more?

Useful organizations

Animal Samaritans
PO Box 154
Bexleyheath
Kent DA16 2WS
tel: 020 8303 1859
www.animalsamaritans.org.uk

Association of Pet Behaviour Counsellors
PO Box 46
Worcester WR8 9YS
tel: 01386 751151
www.apbc.org.uk

Battersea Dogs' Home
4 Battersea Park Road
Battersea
London SW8 4AA
tel: 020 7622 3626
www.dogshome.org

Blue Cross
Shilton Road, Burford
Oxon OX18 4PF
tel: 01993 822651
www.bluecross.org.uk
www.allaboutpets.org.uk

British Veterinary Association
7 Mansfield Street
London W1M 0AT
tel: 020 7636 6541
www.bva.co.uk

Cats Protection
National Cat Centre
Chelwood Gate, Haywoods
Heath, Sussex RH17 7TT
Tel: 08707 708649
Helpline: 08702 099099
www.cats.org.uk

Celia Hammond Animal Trust
High Street
Wadhurst
East Sussex TN5 6AG
tel: 01892 783367
www.celiahammond.org

Cinnamon Trust
10 Market Square
Hayle
Cornwall TR27 4HE
tel: 01736 757900
www.cinnamon.org.uk

The Feline Advisory Bureau
Taeselbury
High Street
Salisbury
Wiltshire SP3 6LD
tel: 0870 7422278
www.fabcats.org

The Governing Council of the Cat Fancy
5 King's Castle Business Park
The Drove, Bridgwater
Somerset
TA6 4AG
tel: 01278 427575
www.gccfcats.org

PDSA (People's Dispensary for Sick Animals)
PDSA House
Whitechapel Way
Priorslee
Telford
Shropshire
TF2 9PQ
tel: 01952 290 999
www.pdsa.org.uk

Pet Care Trust
Bedford Business Centre
170 Mile Road
Bedford MK42 9TW
tel: 08700 624400
email: info@petcare.org.uk
www.petcare.org.uk

Pets as Therapy (PAT)
3 Grange Farm Cottages
Wycombe Road
Saunderton
Princes Risborough
Bucks HP27 9NS
tel: 0870 977 0003
www.petsastherapy.org

Royal College of Veterinary Surgeons
62-64 Horseferry Road
London SW1P 2AF
tel: 020 7222 2001
www.rcvs.org.uk

RSPCA
Wilberforce Way
Southwater
Horsham
West Sussex RH13 9RS
tel: 0870 55 55 999
(cruelty and advice line)
0870 33 35 999
(enquiries service)
www.RSPCA.org.uk

Wood Green Animal Shelters
601 Lordship Lane
Wood Green
London N22 5LG
tel: 08701 904440
www.woodgreen.org.uk

Useful websites

Mayhew Animal Homes
www.mayhewanimalhome.org
email: info@mayhewanimalhome.org
tel: 020 8969 0178
Animal home and education and training centre.

National Animal Welfare Trust
www.nawt.org.uk
Rehoming animals; rescue centres in the UK.

Pet Health Care
www.PEThealthcare.co.uk
Online information on petcare, insurance and
veterinary advice.

Pet Organic
www.petorganic.com
Range of organic and natural pet foods and products.

Pet Planet
www.petplanet.co.uk
Online shopping for wide range of pet products.

Tommy's
www.tommys.org
email: info@tommys.org
tel: 0870 777 3060
Provides information on toxoplasmosis and
support network.

UK Animal Rescuers
www.animalrescuers.co.uk
Comprehensive guide to animal
welfare, rescue centres and
rehoming in the UK.

Feline magazines and publications

Cat World
Ancient Lights
19 River Road
Arundel
West Sussex BN18 9EY
tel: 01903 884988
email: info@catworld.co.uk
www.catworld.co.uk

Our Cats
5 James Leigh Street
Manchester M1 5NF
tel: 0870 731 6505
www.ourcats.co.uk

Your Cat
Roebuck House
33 Broad Street
Stamford
Lincs PE9 1RB
tel: 01780 766199
www.yourcat.co.uk

Further reading

Gair, Angela, *Family Pet Guides: Cat* (Collins)
Heath, Sarah, *Cat and Kitten Behaviour: An Owner's Guide* (Collins)
RSPCA Pet Guide, *Collins Care for Your Cat* (Collins)
RSPCA Pet Guide, *Collins Care for Your Kitten* (Collins)
Taylor, David, *Think Cat* (Cassell)

Index

Abyssinian 24

aggression 14, 18, 25, 35, 46, 63, 100, 101, 118, 120–126

allergies 12, 2, 50

allogrooming 103

anaemia 163, 165

anal region 20, 21, 50, 138

Angora 24

anxiety 110, 118–119, 132

appetite 52, 151, 155, 159

  abnormal 133

arthritis 173

artificial respiration 182

bad breath 142, 150, 151

behaviour 86–135

  hunting 54, 63, 73, 74, 75, 88, 104, 105, 110

  natural 104–105, 110

  problems, curing 110–135

  social 102–103

Birman 24

bleeding 183

blood in faeces 52, 150, 151

blood in urine 157

body language 96–101

body shape 10

breathing 181

  laboured 52, 148

breeders 14

breeds 10

British shorthair 12, 24

Burmese 24, 49, 107

burns 184

car travel 80–81

carry boxes 32, 53, 80, 81

cat flaps 46, 108–109, 116, 121

cat runs 25, 26, 46

cataracts 155

catteries 85

chemicals 38, 150

chimneys 39

choosing a cat 8–29

claws 70, 93, 130, 138

climbing trees 41, 48

coat 10, 11, 50, 52, 64

  grooming 64–69

  markings 15

collars 38, 49, 78, 79

colour 11–12, 15

concussion 172

confrontation 88

constipation 150, 151

coughing 52, 138, 162

cross-breeds 15

deafness 146, 177

dehydration 52, 153

dermatitis 167

diabetes 151, 155

diarrhoea 52, 150, 152, 153

diet 54–57, 71, 72–75, 174–175

displacement grooming 125, 132

dogs 36–37, 106

drinking 52, 72

ear mites 70, 146

ears 20, 51, 52, 53, 70–71, 98, 138, 146–147

eczema 167

elderly cats 155, 156, 173, 174–177

electric cables 38

epilepsy 170–171

exercise 47

eyes 20, 51, 53, 70, 99–100, 138, 144–145, 155, 177, 184

facial signals 97–100

fearfulness 118–119

feeding 54–57, 60, 72–75, 174–175

feline chlamydial infection 149

feline immuno deficiency 153

feline infectious anaemia 164

feline infectious enteritis 153, 165

feline infectious peritonitis 153

feline influenza 145, 147, 148–149, 165

feline leukaemia 164–165

feral cats 27

first aid 180–187

flatulence 151

fleas 20, 52, 53, 67, 140, 162, 166

flehmen response 91

foreign bodies 141, 184

fur balls 64, 68, 150

games 77

garden ponds 41

genetic disorders 145

good cat behaviour 86–135

grooming 10–11, 24, 25, 50, 60, 64–71, 103, 118, 125, 132, 177

gum disease 71, 141

handling 35, 50, 63, 124–125

harvest mites 166

healthcare 13, 20–21, 50–53

heart massage 181

heart problems 162

heart worms 162

heat exhaustion 81

holidays 85

hormonal disease 151

house cats 25, 27, 47, 55–56, 60, 62, 75, 78, 82

house moving 82–84, 134

house plants 40, 131

house training 17, 44–45, 76

hunting 54, 63, 73, 74, 75, 88, 104, 105, 110

hypothermia 81

identification 78–79

indoor safety 38–40

indoor toileting 18, 113, 114–117, 127–129

infertility 158

insecurity 45

intelligence 106

Jacobson's organ 91
kidney disease 151, 156
kittens 14, 16, 30–57, 62
  choosing 20–25
  collecting 32
  exercising 47
  feeding 54–57
  handling 35, 50
  health 20–21, 50–53
  house training 44–45
  neutering 19
  rescue 12
  safety 38–41
  settling in 34
  training 43
  vaccinating 16, 50, 53
  worming 50
lead training 49, 107
lice 166
liquid medicines, giving 178
litter trays 17, 44, 45, 76, 127–129
longhairs 10–11, 24, 25, 62, 64, 65, 132
  grooming 66–69, 177
mad cow disease 171
Maine Coon 24
malabsorption 151
marking 34, 45, 46, 90–91, 94–95, 110, 114–117
meningitis 170
metritis 158–159
microchipping 78
middening 95
mineral deficiency 154
miscarriage 158

mouth 20, 51, 142–143, 176, 184
moving house 82–84, 134
multi-cat households 18, 114, 122, 129
mutual grooming 103
myelitis 171
nervous system diseases 170–172
nervousness 46, 62, 65, 110, 118, 161
nocturnal vision 144
Norwegian Forest Cat 41, 62
nose 21, 51, 138, 147, 184
obesity 154
Orientals 24
outdoor safety 41
overeating 151
over-grooming 118, 132
paralysis 172
parasites 20, 50, 52, 68, 151, 166–169
paws 51
pedigree cats 12, 13
Persian 24, 65
petting and biting syndrome 124
pica 133
picking up cats 63
play 35, 77, 105
poisonous plants 41
poisons 27, 41, 150, 186–187
ponds 41, 72
pregnancy 16, 19, 158–161, 169
pressure points 183
prey 54, 71, 73, 88, 104, 143

prolapse of uterus 159
pulse 181
punishment 44, 62, 117, 119
pyometra 151, 160
queens 19, 24, 54, 158–161
rescue cats 12, 15, 26
respiratory problems 52, 148–149
restraining a cat 179
rewarding good behaviour 43, 62, 63, 106–107, 108, 119
ringworm 167
roundworms 168
rubbing 92, 102
safety 38–41
scent 88, 122
  marking 90–91, 93
  rubbing 92
  scratching 93
  signals 45, 123, 130
scratching 18, 93, 110
  furniture 130
  posts 42–43, 130
self-grooming 64
shock 184
shorthairs 10–11, 24, 25, 60, 62, 64
  grooming 65–66
Siamese 12, 13, 24, 145
skin 120, 138, 166–167
sleep 77
small pets 37
sneezing 52, 147
social interaction 88, 102–103, 119
socialization 14, 18, 19, 24, 112, 118
spraying 14, 16, 19, 24, 45, 46, 94–95, 110,

114–117
straying 134–135
tablets, giving 178
tail 50, 100–101
tapeworms 168
teeth 20, 51, 53, 71, 140, 141–143, 151, 176
third eyelid 20, 145
thirst 155, 157, 159
thrombosis 164
ticks 166, 167
timidity 118–119
toxoplasmosis 169
toys 47–48, 105
training 43, 106–109
travel crates 32, 53, 80, 81
treats 74
tummy problems 150–153
Turkish 24
urinary problems 113, 156–157
urination 18, 44–45, 46, 76, 94–95, 110, 113, 127–129
vaccinations 16, 50, 53, 85, 140, 148, 149, 153, 165
vitamin deficiency 154
vocalization 88
vomiting 52, 150, 151, 152, 153, 159, 165
washing machines 40
water 72
weight 51, 154
  loss 52, 157, 165
windows 38
wool eating 133
worming 50, 52, 53, 140, 168, 169

☽ Collins need to know?

Look out for these recent titles in Collins' practical and accessible need to know? series.

Other titles in the series:

Antique Marks
Aquarium Fish
Birdwatching
Body Language
Buying Property in France
Buying Property in Spain
Calorie Counting
Card Games
Chess
Children's Parties
Codes & Ciphers

Decorating
Detox
Digital Photography
DIY
Dog Training
Drawing & Sketching
Dreams
First Aid
Food Allergies
Golf
Guitar

How to Lose Weight
Kama Sutra
Kings and Queens
Knots
Low GI/GL Diet
Mushroom Hunting
Pilates
Poker
Pregnancy
Property
Speak French

Speak Italian
Speak Spanish
Stargazing
Watercolour
Weddings
Wine
Woodworking
The World
Universe
Yoga
Zodiac Types

To order any of these titles, please telephone **0870 787 1732** quoting reference **263H**.
For further information about all Collins books, visit our website:
www.collins.co.uk